moore ruble yudell making *place*

BUZZ YUDELL & JOHN RUBLE

making *place*

moore ruble yudell

BUZZ YUDELL & JOHN RUBLE

images
Publishing

Published in Australia in 2004 by
The Images Publishing Group Pty Ltd
ACN 059 734 431
6 Bastow Place, Mulgrave, Victoria 3170, Australia
Telephone (61 3) 9561 5544 Fax (61 3) 9561 4860
E-mail: books@images.com.au
Website: www.imagespublishinggroup.com

Ruble, John and Yudell, Buzz.
Moore Ruble Yudell: making place.

Bibliography.
ISBN 1 876907 47 9.

1. Moore, Charles, 1925-1993. 2. Yudell, Buzz.
3. Ruble, John. 4. Architecture, Modern–20th century.
5. Architecture. I. Ruble, John. II. Title.
(Series : Master architect series. VI).

721
Design: Aufuldish & Warinner
Editorial supervision, copy editing, research, and
coordination of project documentation:
Janet Sager and Rebecca Bubenas, Moore Ruble Yudell
Photo archive: Tony Tran, Moore Ruble Yudell
Jacket concept: Ken Kim, Moore Ruble Yudell
Editorial advisor: James Mary O'Connor, Moore Ruble Yudell
Editorial consultant: Wendy Kohn

Co-ordinating editor: Eliza Hope, IMAGES
Production by The Graphic Image Studio Pty Ltd,
Mulgrave, Australia
Film separations by Mission Productions
Printed by Everbest Printing Co. Ltd. in Hong Kong/China

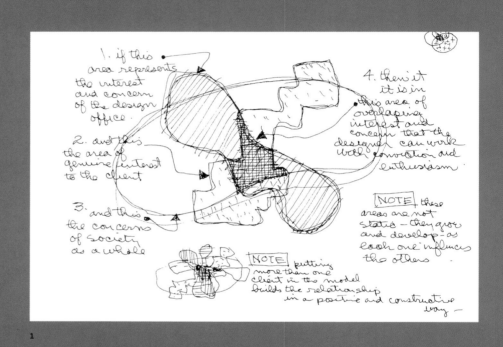

1. if this area represents the interest and concern of the design office.

2. and this the area of genuine interest to the client

3. and this the concerns of society as a whole

4. then it it is in this area of overlapping interest and concern that the designer can work with conviction and enthusiasm.

NOTE these areas are not static — they grow and develop as each one influences the others.

NOTE putting more than one client in this model builds the relationship in a positive and constructive way —

1

Buzz Yudell & John Ruble

THE WORK OF ARCHITECTURE IS DAUNTING AND EXHILARATING. As an applied art, mediated by the forces of time, physicality, and society, its successes and pleasures depend on shared convictions, nurtured gestation, and the confluence of the zeitgeist and the architect's convictions.

Charles Eames captured the complexity of this dynamic process in an exquisite diagram. Three freeform shapes represent the "interest and concern of the design office...the client...and of society as a whole..." He notes "...it is in this area of overlapping interest and concern that the designer can work with conviction and enthusiasm" and importantly that "these areas are not static. They grow and develop as one influences the others" and that "the overlap of more parties only adds to the richness of the creative process" and "builds the relationship in a positive and constructive way." (fig. 1).

Charles and Ray Eames exemplified their embrace of dynamic complexity in the "work-play" of their lives. Yet after some early buildings in St. Louis, a collaboration with Eero Saarinen on the Entenza house and the *gesamtkunstwerk* of their own house, they chose to focus on film, furniture, and exhibition design. They found the highly mediated and less controllable process of making architecture too protracted and frustrating.

In adapting to this rigorous environment, architects have evolved varying mechanisms for nurturing ideas into buildings. Their styles cover the spectrum, from the much-caricatured imperious master to the acquiescent functionary. The reality is much more complex: the most single-minded visionary must connect with a wide array of cultural forces and the most accommodating practitioner must have vision to achieve meaningful architecture.

In our work we have sought to balance a deep understanding of place, society, and client with a passionate exploration of ideas, realized in space and time.

Our work is dependent upon an extended dialogue, which begins with listening and is enriched by collaboration. From our earliest work we were inspired by our partner Charles Moore to expand the circle of collaboration both within our office and into our community.

We explore ways to invite the participation of our clients, to understand the many dimensions of a place, to shape a vision, and to craft an environment which inhabits its site harmoniously and which invites human habitation.

The essence of the buildings we craft emerges from our energetic commitment to understanding, shaping, and inhabiting place.

understanding
shaping
inhabiting

place

Robert Campbell

MY FIRST SERIOUS CONTACT WITH MOORE RUBLE YUDELL OCCURRED IN WASHINGTON IN 1996. I'd long been acquainted with
the firm's senior partner, the celebrated architect Charles W. Moore, but Moore had died three years earlier. John Ruble and Buzz
Yudell were in Washington to present their proposed design for a new American Embassy in Berlin. They were one of six firms, all
nationally known, that the State Department had asked to prepare a design for a critical site next to the Brandenburg Gate. I was a
member of the jury that was to pick the best design and recommend it to the government.

Without a dissenting vote, we picked Moore Ruble Yudell's. Their building was by far the most intelligently organized and by far the
most thoughtfully worked out in detail. But beyond that, it embodied, in ways I won't try to describe in words, metaphors of American
life and culture. It was a building that people would enjoy inhabiting, partying in, working in. It was respectful of its historic surroundings without losing its sense of its own individuality. It was the kind of building we too rarely see today.

We live in an era when the world of architecture is split into two camps. There are the famous avant-garde architects, who dominate
the press with a few buildings of spectacular novelty, buildings that become personal expressions of the architect's talent and
often bring him or her celebrity. The most notable to date is probably the Guggenheim Museum in Bilbao, Spain, by the American
architect Frank O. Gehry. These are often wonderful buildings, and people rightly travel long distances to see them. But at the
same time, few people want their own house, school, or workplace to be designed in a similar style. They resent the rupture with a
familiar language of architecture that they have learned to appreciate. The avant-garde work feels arbitrary to them, without dis-
cernible meaning. That fact leads people to believe that architects possess an entirely different aesthetic from their own. As a
result, they begin to distrust contemporary architects and architecture. They then fall back into the opposite camp. They become
reactionaries, who demand buildings in familiar historic styles. Such buildings, when actually built, nearly always turn out to be
pathetically weak imitations of what were once vital traditions.

Meanwhile, fear of the new leads to an exaggerated desire for the preservation of whatever is old. At times it seems as if the
preservation movement and the environmental movement are the only non-economic values that our society now perceives in architecture. That being so, it's hard to persuade clients to pay for good new architecture, because nobody agrees on what good
architecture is.

What makes Moore Ruble Yudell important in this situation is that, more than almost any other architects, they are in the business
of bridging the gap between the avant-garde and the reactionary. They make buildings that remember the familiar language of
architecture, its roofs and windows and materials, its human scale, its wish to be inhabited, and its respect for context, both cultural

What makes Moore Ruble Yudell important in this situation is that, more than almost any other architects, they are in the business of bridging the gap between the avant-garde and the reactionary.

and physical. They employ a known visual language which, like all languages, is largely made up of conventions. But like good writers who work with a verbal language, they don't simply repeat the past. They never fail to innovate. Sometimes they do this to address circumstances that are new, such as the need in our time to create buildings that are less exploitive of the planet's resources. But at other times they innovate for the sheer joy of invention and surprise—the unexpected gesture that makes a place different and memorable.

Such gestures are important in any art. But they can only be meaningful when they occur against the background of some framework of expectation. The poet Robert Frost once famously said that, for him, writing free verse would be like playing tennis without a net. How would he know when he'd made a good shot? He needed the framework of rhyme and meter, as the tennis player needs a court, a net, and a book of rules. Moore Ruble Yudell are architects in the manner that Frost was a poet. You're always aware of the architectural parentage of their buildings, the known typologies developed over time, the court, and the book of rules. It's against that background that you can read and enjoy their innovations, as they explore, with keen attention, everything that is novel or particular about the circumstance in which the building finds itself—circumstance of site, function, users, culture, construction, symbolic message. They make this point explicitly in their praise of the Portuguese architect Alvaro Siza: "His elemental forms connect to traditional ways of building…and still delight us with their fresh expression."

The Spanish architect José Rafael Moneo, architect of the new Los Angeles Cathedral, is another architect who, like Moore Ruble Yudell, seeks to close the gap between the public and the avant-garde. He speaks of "the importance of a shared language that might go some way to overcoming the wild individualism of today," and in another essay he writes: "The only sensation of reality left for architecture today resides in its history. The world of images provided by history is the only sensible reality that has not been destroyed by scientific knowledge or by society."

Reading the texts by John Ruble and Buzz Yudell for this book, we're struck by the prevalence of gerunds, nouns that end in "-ing" and speak of process, of things still in a state of becoming, rather than of conclusions or products. We read of "shaping, sculpting, gathering, dividing, making, crafting, ordering, manifesting," and many others. It's a way of thinking and writing that ties the firm back to another kind of history, the life of the firm's mentor, Charles Moore. Moore wrote a classic book (with Donlyn Lyndon and Gerald Allen) called *The Place of Houses* that is also filled with gerunds: "enfronting," "inhabiting," and many more. Moore's buildings always give you the sense of being in a state of inquiry and exploration, as if they are on the way to finding their final form but haven't quite got there yet. It's a manner of design that accepts the inhabitant, and what the inhabitant will do to the building, as an equal partner in the design process. Such buildings seem to welcome their future users with open arms. Unlike the work of high-style architects who present you with a finished aesthetic whole, in which you will always feel yourself to be a visitor or even an intruder, the works of Moore, and of Moore Ruble Yudell, seek to be completed by human habitation. Often, indeed, the future inhabitant is engaged much earlier on, as a literal participant in the design process. Like Charles Moore, Ruble and Yudell like to lead charrettes, intense, short creative sessions in which all the people involved in a future building—sometimes including members of the general public, who after all, will have to live with it—work together to generate ideas and discern shared values.

A visit to the Moore Ruble Yudell office in Santa Monica, at this moment of the firm's life, is a visual delight and a metaphor for its architecture. As you open the door you have a straight visual shot through the office to an idyllic California courtyard beyond, a view that is terminated by the far courtyard wall, painted an intense shade of red-orange selected by Tina Beebe, who specializes in color and materials and who gives the firm's work much of its panache. The wall rises as a complementary color above a stand of blue-green agave plants. As you move toward this courtyard, drawn as if by a kind of tropism, you become aware that you are passing through a former industrial loft, with sunlight drifting through bowstring trusses from skylights overhead. The office is, thus, fresh wine in an old bottle, taking advantage of the surprise and pleasure of the juxtaposition in every possible way, much as the firm's new buildings play with the relationships of memory and invention.

"Creation Is a Patient Search," wrote the great architect Le Corbusier in the title of one of his books. John Ruble, Buzz Yudell, and their associates are still engaged in a lifelong search, and the work is still evolving. Recent projects seem calmer and crisper than in the past, more confident, less theatrical, and less dependent on literal references to historic styles. Now 55, the partners are, in all likelihood, entering the best years of their practice.

listening

reading

mapping

extrapolating

interpolating

collaborating

1 understanding *place*

city
country
region
culture
workshops
context
old and new
process
implementation
places
program
purpose
circulation

connections
typologies
light
land
constraints
family
community

BEGINNING IS A PRECIOUS STATE. The opportunity to approach a project with open and fresh perceptions is critical to its thoughtful and responsive evolution.

In Japan the first time one experiences a phenomenon it is of such special import that it is signified by its own word. The first love, *hatsukoi*, can happen only once in a lifetime. *Hatsu-hibari*, the first skylark, is a season-word for spring. The first snow, *hatsu-yuki*, can only be experienced once each year. The first taste of a food is sanctified with its unique word.

When we begin a project, we try to listen, to be open, to use all the senses. This applies equally to the physical phenomena of site, climate, and senses as to the cultural context of client, program, process, and society. An exploration of architectural typologies and precedents further informs our understanding, while manifesting the intersection of the physical and cultural.

As Christian Norberg-Schulz notes, in *Genius Loci: Towards a Phenomenology of Architecture*, the *genius loci*, or spirit of place, reflects the cultural, phenomenal, climatic, and tectonic uniqueness of landscapes and buildings.

Such threads of place and culture weave through time and space. Understanding them is essential to our ability to create places that connect to their landscapes and culture even as they explore new expressions. This making of places is specific and connected, not generic and rootless.

Place

Context has become a weighted word. Throughout the style wars of modernism, postmodernism, and neomodernism, the import of context has fluctuated wildly. The pure object orientation of much modernism has minimized the concern for context and the conservatism of historicized architecture has taken context as a

2

3

4

constraining condition. Both characterizations are limiting and, as with most labels, undermine our chance to see freshly.

We see site and context as an opportunity to understand a place in a moment of time and as part of a cultural matrix. Understanding and reading a site includes unlocking its physical and societal history in both short and long term timeframes. Through this we can find meaningful relationships whereby we can connect new pieces in space and time. These connections need not be about style. By connecting to how people have marked and inhabited their environments, we can support and extend their relationships to their environments and communities.

We have had the chance to explore these connections in many diverse ecologies. Listening, sensing, and reading these places have been central to our successfully responding in varied situations, from urban infill to rural agricultural sites.

Culture and Program

Architecture and landscape are inevitably the manifestation of deep cultural forces. As architects and planners we can never fully know the complexity of these underlying influences. The dimensions of the cultural context are immense and deeply embedded. However, an effort to be open to the cultural foundations of a place is critical to meaningful architectural initiatives.

To begin our engagement, we start with listening. We listen to the multiple constituencies: both the clients and other communities with strong interests. We engage in dialogue about their needs and aspirations. We try creatively to challenge preliminary assumptions about programmatic needs so that we are not relying on facile assumptions about what elements and relationships can make the most resonant buildings and urban places.

Places that we admire have a strong correlation between the ethos of the culture and the physical development of the architecture, urban form, and landscape. Those places representing older, less fluid cultures are often easier to comprehend and admire.

In the traditional Balinese village the form of the settlement represents the shared understanding of the order of the universe, the nature of the community, and even the structure of the family. A long axis establishes the spine of the community on a line between the dangers of the sea below and the sacred domain of the mountains and heavens above. Communal activities occur at a mid-point. Each residence has a strong presence on the street, marked by a portal that connects laterally to a series of pavilions. These are shaped and built to house and express the individual activities and meanings of life, from eating and sleeping to entertaining and honoring one's ancestors. Here, form follows function as much as in any modern structure (fig. 2). But it goes beyond Sullivan's dictum so that function includes the full hierarchy of cultural meanings.

In contemporary society it is imprudent, if not arrogant, to attempt singular and comprehensive solutions for complex cultural contexts. Indeed most utopian solutions have yielded cultural dystopias. Brasilia and Chandigarh, for all their bold expression and exuberance, are noted for the disjunction between their architectural ambition and the reality of community life, which has struggled to take hold in the shadows of the individual architectural monuments. While the complexities and tensions of contemporary society have challenged our abilities as architects to engage our energies with freshness and meaning, the occasional successes stand in high relief.

Alvaro Siza has found an austere but poetic voice, which connects with and extends the culture of his country. With a minimalist modern palette he evokes the proud quiet elegance of the place and people. His elemental forms connect to traditional ways of building, are animated in the dry light landscape, and still delight us with their fresh expression. He has been able to express this cultural richness both in buildings such as his *Vila do Condo* bank and in ensembles such as his *Quinta de Maqueria* urban housing in Evora, Portugal (fig. 3).

Another poet of cultural expression is the Italian architect Renzo Piano, who has been able to achieve the remarkable feat of connecting meaningfully in countries throughout the world. The Menil Collection, the museum of his design in Houston, produces an almost sacred exhibition space inside, tempering the intense Texas sun, while expressing a modest elegance and scale totally sympathetic to its residential neighborhood of wooden bungalows (fig. 4). This is a feat whose mastery requires a deep understanding of function, culture, and context. His government center in Nouméa, New Caledonia (fig. 5) accomplishes an even bolder task of extrapolating from indigenous building typologies while achieving a complex new expression of construction, climatic and programmatic response and symbolism.

5

In an architectural culture that still fluctuates between the less satisfying polarities of individual icons or nostalgic recapitulations, it is challenging to shape a path that can meaningfully connect to place and culture while expressing and engaging contemporary life.

Typology and Invention

We find the understanding of building types to be a powerful corollary to the exploration of place, program, and culture. Typology can be looked at in a variety of ways: as the taxonomy of pure building forms or *formats*—answers waiting for a question; as a body of architectural ideas that incorporates the deeper purposes of an institution, such as the library or the museum; or as an array of formal themes to be played out in endless variations. To understand type is to look for the deeper or more defining patterns of order and form, as well as to appreciate the particular differences among individual examples.

Some building types teach us about plan arrangements and systems of order. Laboratories, for example, stress the discipline of dimensions, patterns of structure, and careful relations with natural light. But all building types have their poetic, experiential dimension as well. The church or temple, which is about gathering, the rhythms of the liturgy, and celebration, leads directly to more three-dimensional aspects of form: how a roof supports the congregation's sense of unity, for example, and nurtures the presence of light as an ally of the human spirit.

Through the work of Louis Kahn we have come to understand more deeply the elemental, phenomenal essence of particular forms: his famous description of the moment of the individual reader taking a book to the light, and therefore the finer grained texture of spaces within the library; the form of the museum and its devotion to the presence of light, and the procession of movement centered along axes of light (fig. 6).

6

The study of housing types is of profound interest in understanding how architectural form participates in the making of places. The European townhouse with its workplace on the street level and dwelling above, the North African courtyard house that conceals a world of activity behind a wall, the multistory factory or warehouse loft, removed from its original use and available for modern reinterpretation as a dwelling—each of these examples of type bundles a dense intersection of cultural, economic, technological, and aesthetic virtues, the very virtues we want to know about in understanding place.

The inventive pairing of programs of activity with unrelated building types confers very special meaning or "spin" to the activity, which can heighten our awareness of both the form and the (not) related function. Loft housing is our most ubiquitous example. Thomas Jefferson's use of the Roman Pantheon as a form for the Library at the University of Virginia was a multi-layered statement about the freedom and independence of the place of learning; it was, after all, a "pagan" temple, but also a soaring space to inspire the imagination and empower the pursuit of enlightenment.

With a diverse practice that has moved rapidly into new kinds of programs, we have come to appreciate how building typology informs the understanding of program and use. Within the heritage of building forms that have evolved around particular kinds of activities, we can find a wealth of accumulated wisdom, and a source of legibility and clarity of purpose for the building's inhabitants. But our interest in types is not particularly historical; the flipside of typology is invention, the ongoing defining and redefining of form and purpose. Building types will continue to evolve, even radically, as new programs and innovations occur; we see such innovation as enriching, not negating, the great typological inventions of the past.

University of Washington, Tacoma Master Plan
Tacoma, Washington

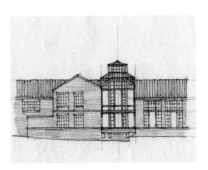

Downtown Tacoma mounts a hilly peninsula looking over Commencement Bay at the southern edge of Puget Sound—it could be called a hill town. The hill towns loved by architects—mostly in Italy or France—are shaped for the pedestrian, with gently climbing, winding streets and tightly gathered buildings. American hill towns are different—the typical, real estate-driven grid of streets is arbitrarily draped over the topography, resulting in some streets dramatically plunging down the hill, and in good examples like San Francisco, providing breathtaking views to waterfronts and distant landscapes.

With less exciting results, Tacoma's grid does much the same, with streets parallel to the slopes closely spaced, and the up/down streets less frequent, setting up a staircase of long rectangular blocks, which in most areas of downtown are only partially built up. The experience of place is melancholy: views of each day's weather between scattered, shadowless buildings present shifting gray and white mists over gray waters. But one part of Tacoma now blooms with color and life: buildings and activities are gathering, and the inconveniently tiered streets are becoming inhabited. At the center of this resurgence of urban life is a campus—a new academic community in an old commercial neighborhood.

An Urban Campus with an Open Future
In the late 1980s, the University of Washington sought to reach out to new populations of students in the Puget Sound region. A site south of Tacoma's downtown was identified for a new campus, and quickly gained support from the City. Comprising just eight of Tacoma's large city blocks, and some 46 acres, the area includes most of the city's historic warehouse district, with a remarkable collection of brick and timber loft buildings in the late 19th-century industrial vernacular. With its steep east-facing slope, parallel to the street grid, dramatic views out to Commencement Bay and nearby Mount Rainier, and railroad tracks cutting diagonally through, the site is a challenging and rich urban environment within which to create a place of learning and culture.

Dimensions of a Found Place
As we began work it was clear that the character and quality of the site would determine the nature of this unique urban campus. As the University's program evolved, it too had special needs as a start-up institution with interdisciplinary approaches and an older student population. For the Campus Master Plan to realize the potential of this extraordinary place, the underlying analysis was the most critical part of the design process. >>>>

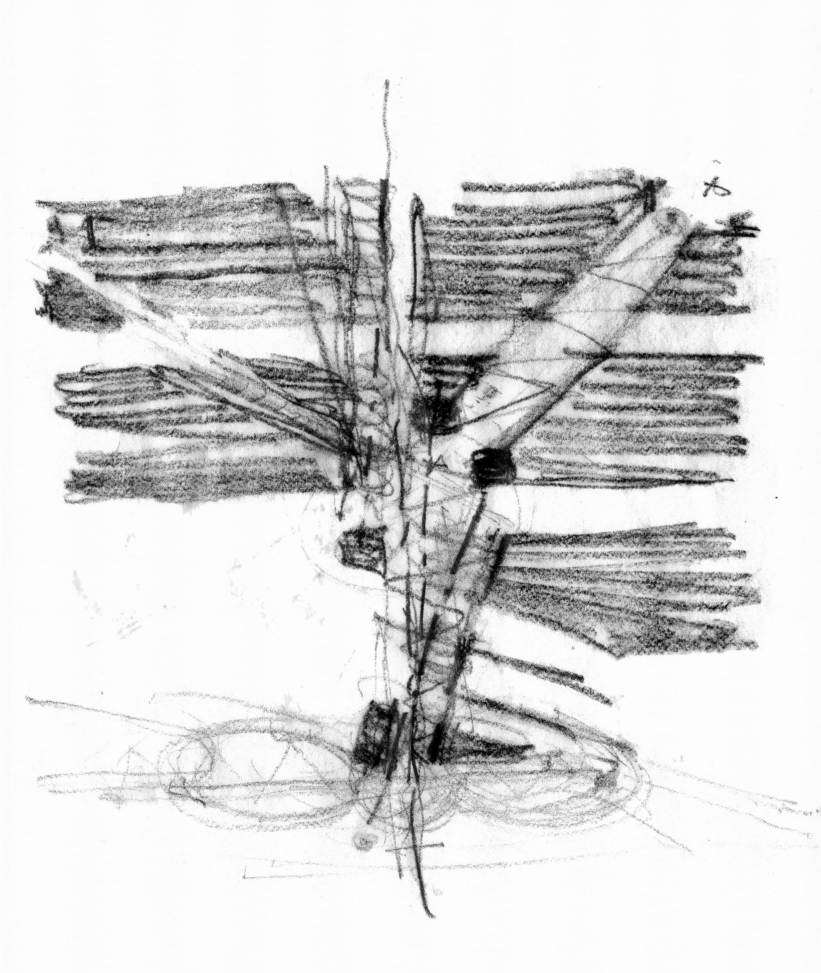

Industrial old and new: Snoqualmie Power
Substation at the center of the warehouse
district.

The new Science Building winter garden.

Science Building plans.

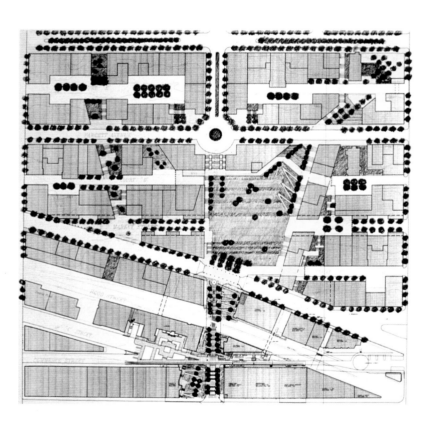

The campus plan is shaped by the urban grid,
site topography, and visual axes.

Pacific Gateway Plaza begins a sequence of stairways and terraced gardens moving up the hill.

Analysis of the site proceeded on three levels simultaneously. Moore Ruble Yudell's team studied a range of urban and environmental issues, from climate conditions to geography to urban infrastructure and context. Our associates at LMN Architects surveyed and carefully evaluated the condition of the neighborhood's stock of historic structures. Buster Simpson, a well-known Tacoma artist consulting with our team, developed a visual study of the district from a phenomenological viewpoint, focusing on the artifacts of industrial technology as found. From our studies, and intense discussions about their implications for planning, we established a number of principles:

· Street Grid: In order to link the campus visually to the City, the street grid would be maintained—not always for vehicular traffic, but as a formal framework for buildings and open space.
· Mix of Uses: The Campus would evolve as a mixed-use, pedestrian-oriented district, in which the University would allow for commercial and appropriate neighborhood-serving uses.
· Inside-Outside: The edges of the eight-block square campus would be given identity through urban landscape treatment, with significant gateways leading into the center.

· Public Space: As an armature for the pedestrian network, a series of major green spaces would provide an academically oriented public realm centered on a grand, terraced wedge of park using regional landscape materials.
· View Axes: A chosen set of visual axes based on existing local and regional landmarks would cut through the urban grid, in several directions up and down the hillside, helping to pull together the campus as it grows over many phases.
· Adaptive Re-use: The initial phases of the Campus would modify and re-use the warehouse buildings, with limited new construction clearly distinguished from historical fabric.

Reshaping the Industrial Loft

As we proceeded to implement the 1992 Master Plan, two interesting developments emerged. Re-use of the warehouse lofts became a process of typological reinvention: the centers of the blocky buildings were carved out, providing sky-lit atria to enhance vertical circulation and natural light. The old loading docks along Commerce Street were rebuilt as continuous student porches, connecting classrooms and the street.

Three-Dimensional Pedestrian Network

Another unique feature of the campus emerged in response to topography. Stepped gardens and inclined paths barely solved accessibility on the steep grade, and in Phase 2 we began to implement a more radical strategy: a series of connected bridges and winter-garden lobbies link the campus circulation to building elevators, producing a hybrid interior-exterior pedestrian network that climbs up the hill. In response to these site-specific demands, we have had to create an environment with a pattern of interior social spaces, visually connected to the outside, which also fits Tacoma's cool, damp climate.

Campuses are the settings for a special kind of community, with an enduring sense of purpose that transcends changing times and transient populations. The moment of their foundation, and the "place where it all began" hold important meanings. At the Tacoma Campus this is secured through the careful adaptation of the warehouse district, giving this fledgling institution a depth of character that belies its age, and a core of distinct buildings and spaces to inspire future architecture and place-making.

Commerce Street: North-south streets provide "landings" on the hillside and visual links to downtown.

Library Square: New structures, like the lantern, help re-establish the warehouse district as a place of learning.　　>>>>

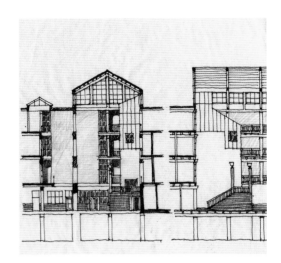

A pattern of interior social spaces, visually
connected to the outside.

Industrial hall as library reading room.

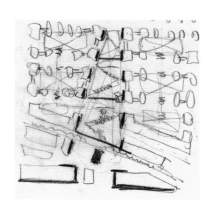

Tiergarten Dreieck
Berlin, Germany

The Dreieck—triangle—is a trapezoidal city block wedged like a key stone between the Landwehr Kanal and the Tiergarten, Berlin's celebrated central park. Its district is an elegant mix of embassies, art galleries, and up-market residential, all buffered from the surrounding city by flowing green spaces. In the eighties, Rob Krier had built the Rauch Strasse—a fine collection of multi-unit "urban villas" embracing a lovely garden court—just around the corner, and it may have served as a model for the Tiergarten Dreieck's master plan by Machleit and Stepp. The neighboring Scandinavian Embassy complex is a newer collection of distinguished modern buildings drawn tightly together by an undulating wall of patinated copper.

Perforated Urban Blocks
The particular pattern of block development that these successful works all share is a variation on the typical Berlin block. Berlin blocks are often large—more than 100 meters square—enclosed by contiguous six-story houses. In the Tiergarten variation the enclosure is broken into separate buildings spaced closely together. The Tiergarten Dreieck's plan features 6-meter-wide lanes between small office or residential buildings, leading into a central garden, which serves as an amenity for residents, and is also open to the public during business hours.

Collective Character
As one of several architects invited to design for this up-scale setting, we were assigned a site for an office building adjacent to the new Mexican Embassy, as well as a portion of a residential court on the Kanal. All the buildings would share a palette of warm sandstone and plaster walls, with metal roofs and wood windows, reinforcing the sense that each building should be seen as part of a larger whole. Most of the design teams agreed on a "second look" architecture— a more quiet character revealing deeper qualities each time it is seen. Exceptions are the Mexican Embassy, a handsome, sculptural work by Teodoro Gonzales Gerardo e Leon, and the Christian Democratic Party Headquarters, which looks like a dry-docked tug boat in a glass box.

Sustainable Workplace
The small, nearly square footprint of our building site was not optimum for office use in Germany, where daylight and view requirements for offices lead to long, narrow wings. We made the best of the plan by wrapping workplaces around a south-facing atrium. While in design, our office building became the headquarters for the Association of German Savings Banks, who found the atrium useful for exhibitions and gatherings. They also wanted a technologically flexible space, with raised floors and modular partitions, as well as daylight-activated controls for office lighting. Sustainability is much more the standard in Germany, and guided the choices of interior and exterior materials, such as the sedum-covered roof.

The second-look design of our office building seems at first to be a typical postwar Berlin scheme of horizontal bands of windows and stone spandrels. Its soul and the viewer's reward lie in the careful joinery of its wood, stainless steel, and sandstone façade, animated by an off-center oriel of glass and steel, and a glassy rooftop conference room looking out over the Tiergarten.

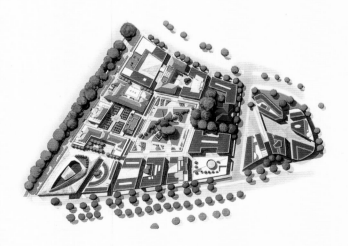

The office building wraps flexible workspace
around a small atrium.

The Peg Yorkin House
Malibu, California

This house evolved in response to the tensions of its site, on the edge of a city that sees itself as the edge of the continent. Along the eastern border of the site, the Pacific Coast Highway carries streams of commuters and leisure traffic with their attendant noise, speed, and auto-induced adrenaline. The Santa Monica Mountains end abruptly east of the PCH. They provide the threat of seasonal fires, a cacophony of new houses since the fire of 1993, and the fragile allure of the indigenous landscape. The western edge of the site is the sandy beach of the Pacific with stunning and infinitely transforming panoramas. Tightly fit between these two intense habitats is the Yorkin house, designed to provide refuge for three generations of a family sustained by creative work and social activism.

Matrix of Family Life
The house serves as a social and familial retreat for the owner, her two adult children and their families, all of whom were intimately involved in the design process. It was critical for the house to accommodate one person or many with equal comfort, and to support a full spectrum of activities from formal to informal, throughout all seasons. This dense program led to an urban courtyard house typology, a matrix of spaces overlaid with a system of sliding glass and interior panels to provide varying degrees of community and privacy and a range of openness to the environment.

Outside/Inside
The house mediates between dissonant realms, and unfolds as a series of layers that allows for decompression from the intense car culture outside. Entry is through a courtyard of native beach grasses and over a wooden boardwalk. Once inside, the layers progress from more internally focused family areas to open, light-filled social spaces that communicate through sliding glass walls to an exterior courtyard, terrace, and beach beyond. Stairs weave vertically through this layering to bring color, light, and openness from above. The roof is developed and expressed as a collection of light scoops and terraces which culminate the vertical spatial movement.

The house expresses the dualities of its site. It is solid and urban on the highway, transparent and transformable toward the water, and permeable and vertically connected to the light and sky.

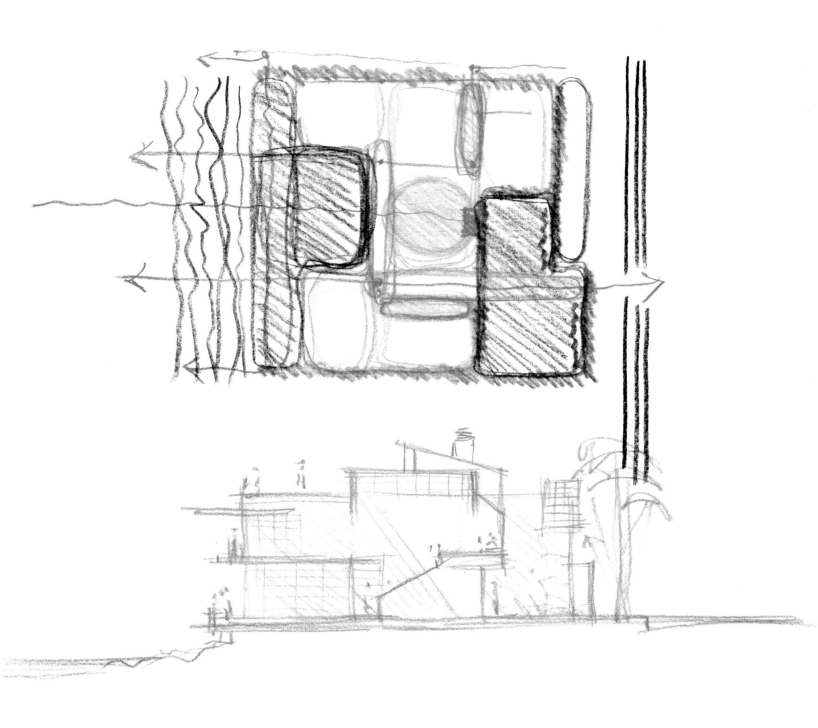

Layered space and light mediate the inside-
outside continuum.

*The typology of urban courtyard house was overlaid with
a system of sliding glass and interior panels to provide
varying degrees of community and privacy and a range
of openness to the environment.*

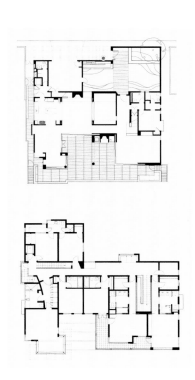

Intimate porches and sitting areas provide
projected outlooks to the land and sea.

Dartmouth College North Campus Master Plan
Hanover, New Hampshire

Dartmouth College has a particularly beautiful and intact natural and built heritage, but its sensitive environment faces special challenges as new building types and diminishing developable land threaten the delicate balance of building and landscape.

A primal, rural landscape of a forested valley along the north-south corridor of the Connecticut River continues to inform the essence and experience of the college community. A pattern of unimpeded north-south movement along the valley and slower east-west movement across slopes characterizes the whole state of New Hampshire including, in fractal fashion, the town of Hanover and the campus.

Common Green
Dartmouth is the only New England campus where college and town have framed and shared an original town "green" from inception to the present.

The bold act of clearing the forest to create the green and then enfronting that figure with individual buildings still resonates more than 200 years later.

Still the center of community, the Green is a powerful yet informal landscape. It is flexible in accommodating varied paths and activities, yet iconic enough to serve as the place for solemn gatherings.

Buildings: Platonic and Pragmatic
The college and its consulting planner Lo-Yi Chan have shown great care in analyzing the patterns of campus development. Buildings have, until recently, remained simply shaped, carefully scaled Platonic forms in the landscape. These are aligned with paths and streets, but do not form walls of buildings. They allow both formal and informal movement throughout the campus. Their taut, classical construction is at once refined and pragmatic.

Recent buildings, whether academic or residential, have accommodated much larger footprints, challenging not only the physical character of the campus but also its social and academic qualities.
>>>>

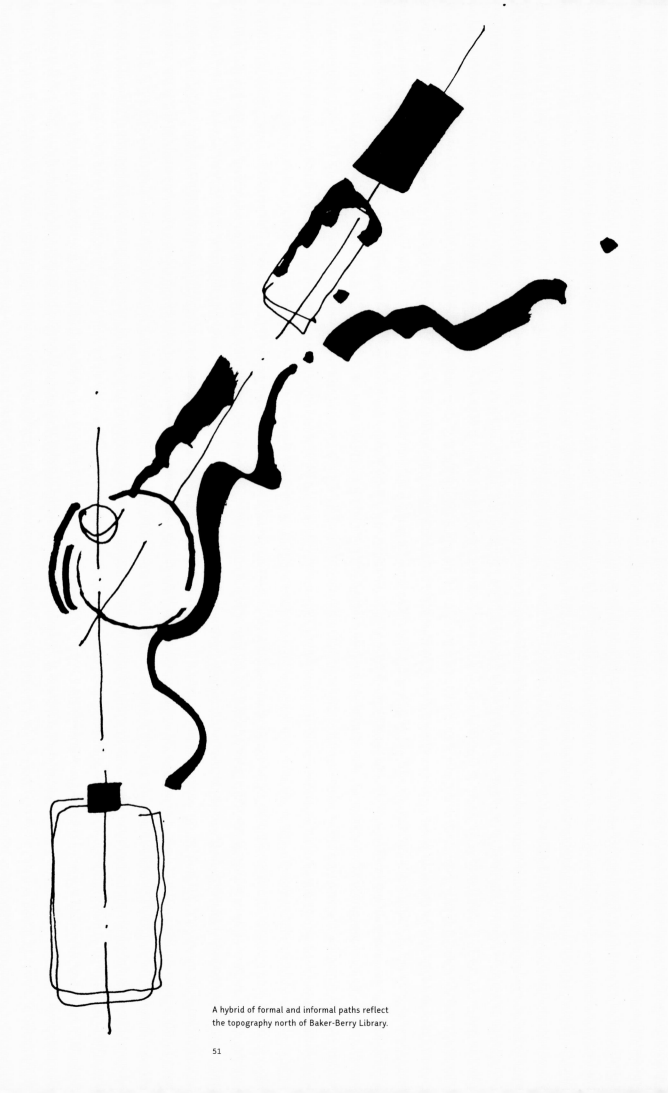

A hybrid of formal and informal paths reflect
the topography north of Baker-Berry Library.

51

The forested landscape along the Connecticut River informs the topography and experience of this college community.

Character and Collegiality

Dartmouth is proud of being an intimate, informal, and nurturing place, which can still compete on the highest level of research and education.

It is a place of true collegiality, which supports interdisciplinary work and informal student-faculty interaction. It is a place where the preservation and enjoyment of the physical environment is integral to student education. These qualities are inextricably bound to the scale, proportions, and expression of the buildings and landscape.

Principled Growth

Our master planning for the area of the Campus north of the central college library rests on several key principles:

· Respect the natural topographies that remain from the primal "valley" morphology.
· Allow for both formal axial and informal transverse movements to support the historic campus patterns.
· Configure new larger buildings both to align with existing streets and to allow for multiple informal site movements.
· Configure new buildings as aggregations of appropriately scaled and simply shaped forms.

Applying these principles in concert with massing and site capacity studies, we have developed a three-dimensional framework for phased development to accommodate contemporary program and site needs, while extending the environmentally and culturally unique qualities which have been central to Dartmouth's ethos.

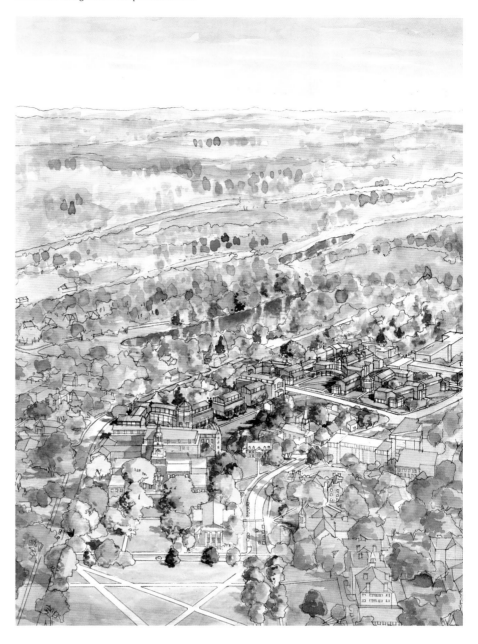

An armature for growth allows for phased
building in harmony with the existing context.

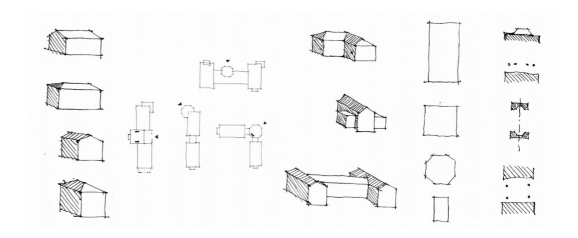

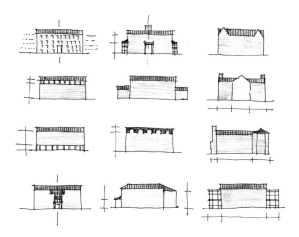

Elemental forms can be aggregated to shape appropriately scaled buildings.

Dartmouth is the only New England campus where college and town have framed and shared an original town "green" from inception to the present.

Formal axial and informal transverse movements support the historic campus patterns.
‹‹‹‹

Interdisciplinary Sciences Building and
Physical Sciences Building
University of California, Santa Cruz

The University of California at Santa Cruz is gloriously sited, overlooking the Monterey Bay on a south-facing hillside that is half meadow and half dense redwood forest. The forest, though grand, is recent—the original timber was cut for fuel to process lime from the calcium-rich "karst" geologic formation that underlies much of the slope. Campus planning has long protected most of the meadow, and the campus has been developed as an archipelago of villages carved out of the woods. Groups of buildings, organized as colleges, establish small clearings—pools of daylight that seem to float in the shadows, linked by damp, winding pathways and occasional bridges. Views of the Bay are rare.

Environmental Adaptation
Somewhere near the middle of the campus is Science Hill, a collection of massive concrete laboratory buildings

for research and teaching, with a handsome Science Library by Esherick, Holmsey, Dodge and Davis. To site new programs on Science Hill is to make buildings as closely shaped to their environment as creatures in a rainforest. Formal or purely geometric architectural schemes quickly morph in response to circumstances. The plan of our Interdisciplinary Sciences Building, which adds offices and classrooms to an existing lab block, is both compact and articulated, its small courts, bays, and corners bump around and between clusters of trees, the shapes of the land, and the surrounding roads. Like a tree on a cliff, the ISB holds tightly to its limited territory while reaching out for light. Greenhouses and planting beds cover most of the roof.

Cutting Paths of Light
Sliding up through the steep elevation of the ISB site is a stair-atrium-courtyard sequence that provides daylight and movement between the two buildings while connecting previously isolated terraces and walks. This kind of linking is of particular urgency on the Santa Cruz campus. Our second project on Science Hill, the Physical Sciences Building, uses a former parking lot, a residual shape among the trees, as it marks an entrance to the Sciences along the main drive. PSB makes its own contribution to the

campus pedestrian network with a top-lit interior street—an axis of light through the site.

Tuning the Envelope
PSB's three-story atrium sets up a multi-level community center for the students and science faculty—a mix of chemists and environmental toxicologists—and negotiates air quality and temperature between heavily air-conditioned labs on one side and naturally ventilated offices on the other. The campus policy at UCSC prohibits mechanical cooling for human comfort, influencing buildings to adapt ever more closely to site and climate. PSB's upper floor spaces at south and west elevations have sun-shaded openings; north elevations—where the labs are—have glassy walls open to the soft light, and provide a beacon in the dark woods at night.

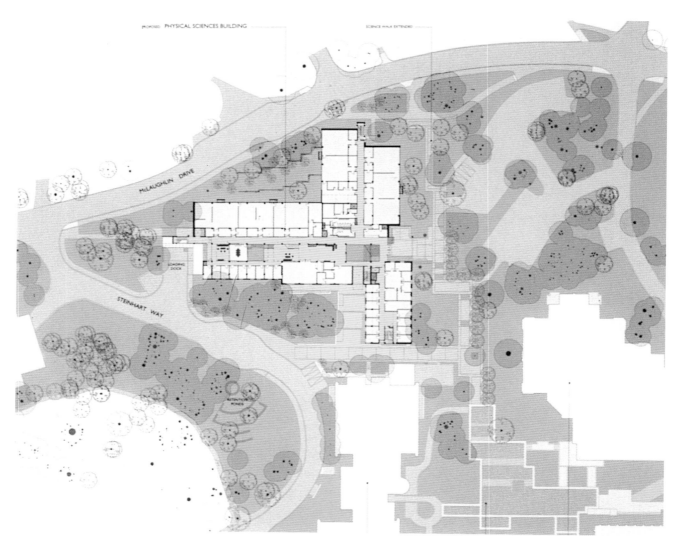

The Physical Sciences Building features a
top-lit interior street as an axis of light
through the site.

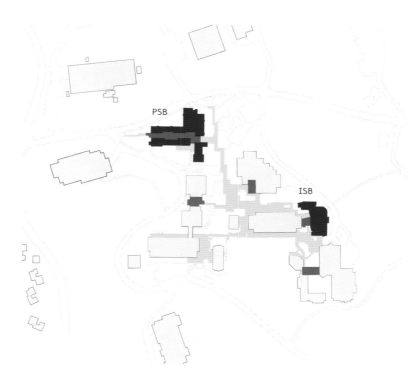

Science Hill's atria, walks, and terraces form
a social network.

The Interdisciplinary Sciences Building
opens to a small sunny courtyard on its
heavily wooded site.

ISB's atrium stair is a place of communication.

The MIT East Campus: Sloan School of Management, the Department of Economics, the School of Humanities and Social Sciences, and the Dewey Library
Cambridge, Massachusetts

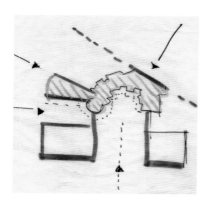

This design effort involved planning for the phased growth of key academic elements, which currently inhabit a compact and somewhat incoherent district at the east end of the campus. Planning spans scales and issues, from the clarifying of faculty research clusters to the shaping of clear building and open space relationships.

The relationships between academic departments will be strengthened, as will the connections to the greater MIT campus and to the city of Cambridge.

Understanding Place
The MIT Campus is part of a dense urban fabric, which is woven into the historic development of Cambridge and metropolitan Boston. The campus occupies an isosceles triangle with a long east-west axis aligned along the Charles River and a short north-south axis defined by Massachusetts Avenue. The intersection of two historic street grids underlies the campus form.

A study led by Laurie Olin resulted in the "Framework Plan," which identified patterns of campus development and clarified principles for growth. Building on this, and collaborating with Sasaki Associates, we identified key opportunities to strengthen visual, spatial, and social linkages between the growing eastern district and the Institute as a whole, as well as to the surrounding city of Cambridge and Boston across the Charles River.

The study area is densely impacted by utilities, dysfunctional buildings, surface parking, disaggregated open space, and minimal connections to the banks of the Charles River.

At the same time, the campus requires the opportunity to phase development to a significantly higher density than now exists in the district and in much of the campus.

By phasing the removal of secondary buildings with the denser development of carefully configured new mixed-use buildings, we proposed a major new campus-serving open space and a revived multi-departmental district.

Supporting Community
The culture of MIT is both informal and intense. Collaboration within and across disciplines is nurtured. At the Sloan School there is a strong initiative to encourage diverse and non-traditional forms of research and study. The intensity of the individual and group work dynamic makes it critical that the architecture can support the multiple interactions that enhance their community. Multiple scales of community must be supported; from two individuals interacting, to whole departments meeting, to connecting to the campus community at large.

Building Types and Precedents
Among the earliest buildings on the campus, the Main Group of the Bosworth Buildings is an elegant set of neoclassical blocks, which form major and minor quads with strong relationships to the Charles River. These buildings project a tough, uncomplicated vitality. Within each building, circulation is clear and bi-axial. The concrete structural frame is expressed inside. There is a no-nonsense discipline and elegance, which has helped these buildings to serve and thrive throughout the decades. >>>>

The building links existing and new elements,
creating a new focus at the eastern end of the
MIT campus.

63

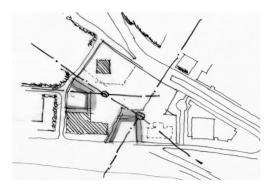  

Their loft-like interiors have been serially renovated to meet shifting needs. Their ample corridors have become major campus circulation, information, and meeting spaces.

Subsequent new buildings have expressed varied approaches: unpretentious lofts, undistinguished laboratories often located with little effort to help shape the public realm, and the occasional architectural icon (Saarinen's chapel and auditorium, Pei's towers, Aalto's Baker House).

The simple lofts and a few icons (especially Baker House) are the most cherished buildings on campus. There has been much ambivalence about strongly iconic buildings. In recent years William Mitchell, Dean of the School of Architecture, and Charles Vest, President of the University, have worked hard to reconcile architectural excellence with thoughtful and informed campus planning. Laurie Olin has led the planning effort and such architects as Gehry, Maki, Holl, and Correa have designed ambitious buildings with a much greater understanding of how powerful architecture can also contribute to the shaping of a rich and coherent campus.

Of Lofts and Links

Our plan for the East Campus is organized around the shaping of major new campus open spaces. The new buildings act to frame those spaces as well as to incubate academic interaction. At the urban scale, major paths, new buildings, and open spaces are organized along the key axes of the campus and the city. Their form and spatial experience reference the intersection of the historic street grids.

The current plan accommodates a mix of academic and social spaces in more than 500,000 square feet. Some 200 units of housing can be accommodated in later phases to support long-term institutional goals.

The Phase One building is organized as a horizontally and vertically integrated community. The first two floors accommodate instructional and social spaces and function as campus and departmental links. They connect continuously to a strongly figured entry court and to the river-facing quad. They allow for linkages to a matrix of existing academic buildings.

A series of loft-like towers rise from these more public spaces. They are configured to encourage interaction in optimally sized faculty clusters oriented to different areas of research. These can, in turn, link horizontally through "soft boundaries" and vertically through social stairs. A new library is woven into this community fabric, strategically located at the intersection of major paths and site geometries. It serves adjacent departments and the Institute as a whole.

Through the shaping of path and place at multiple scales, the overall plan seeks to create a new multi-departmental focus for research, instruction, and community interaction.

The clear new figure-ground plan should establish a strong connection to the greater campus and a vital presence at its eastern prow.

The school's academic interactions are
enhanced by physical paths and connections.

> *"To build a dwelling is to construct a place in which the*
> *inhabitants can be most truly themselves."*
>
> —E.G. Benswanger

Dwelling at 225 Alvarado Road

Stephen Walrod

THE ALVARADO ROAD HOUSE IN BERKELEY WAS BUILT TO REPLACE A TUDOR-STYLE
HOME THAT MY FAMILY HAD LIVED IN FOR 16 YEARS UNTIL IT BURNED TO THE
GROUND IN THE BERKELEY/OAKLAND FIRESTORM OF 1991. On a sunny February
morning my wife and I ventured out of Berkeley for the first time since the fire to
visit MRY. Buzz Yudell met us at the Santa Monica office, showed us slides and models of the firm's work, and asked us about the kind of house that we had in mind;
then we drove up the coast to his and Tina Beebe's home in Malibu.

My first sensation upon entering the house was an olfactory one—of homemade
tomato soup stewing on the stove. We entered the home from the top of a gently
sloping site, with coastal hills to our backs and the ocean beckoning in the distance.
Once inside, my gaze was drawn down a cascading series of limestone stairs and
landings, each with an adjacent living space to one side and views of the garden to
the other. Below and beyond my eye traveled over a hedge of blossoming iceberg
roses and the smooth, reflective surface of the swimming pool, to the ethereal Pacific Ocean in the distance. I breathed a deep sigh of relief.

Playing against this powerful mountain-to-sea axis was the invitation to ascend,
issued by the minimalist yet muscular staircase to the left of the entrance. "What is
up there?" I wondered. I climbed the stairs to discover a long book-lined hallway.
Passing a romantic bedroom with a covered balcony, narrower stairs took me higher,
terminating in a tiny tower office space with a panoramic view of both hills and
ocean. "This house has magic," I thought.

The house was sensual, intelligent, humanistic, but most importantly to me at that
time, it was serene—quietly glowing in the afternoon Pacific coast light. This was the
kind of dwelling that we wanted for our new home. Buzz, John Ruble, Tina and the
MRY group listened, discussed, and designed a home for us that had all of the qualities of the Yudell/Beebe home while at the same time responding to our particular

needs. I expressed an interest in turn-of-the-century Viennese architecture, which led to a Wiener Werkstatte-inspired metal railing and a Klimtian silver decorative ceiling detail. A burgundy check pattern tucked under the eaves related the house to its neighbor across the street, designed by the Berkeley architect Bernard Maybeck.

An exterior palette of sage green, pale yellow, and gray was selected because it was better suited to the northern California landscape than the terracotta typically found in southern California.

The house was constructed with natural, elemental materials: a metal roof; slate decks; maple flooring; limestone mantels; stained wooden ceilings; and thick, hand-trowelled, integral color plaster walls. The dimensions and proportions of the spaces shift as one moves through the house, experiencing a carefully choreographed sequence of transitions: tall to short, wide to narrow, cozy to grand, high to low. I feel contained but never confined, always connected to the outside, to the gardens, to the California light.

I am at ease in the house in part due to the consistent patterns that integrate diverse elements in the house at every scale. At the same time, I experience surprise, whimsy, and more than a touch of magic in features such as a tower within a tower reachable only by climbing a ladder, or a window seat on the lowest level of the house where I can nap, read, or gaze out past a climbing rose to a small lily pond. More than anything, what makes it hard for me to leave for work in the morning, often draws me back for lunch at midday, and beckons me at dusk, is the serenity, first experienced at Buzz and Tina's house in Malibu and now on Alvarado Road. That feeling is worth more to me than the "Oh my God!" effect typically sought by other architects.

ordering

dividing

gathering

carving

extending

connecting

II shaping
place

vision   pavilion
form   cosmology
integration   accident
elegance   inside
geometry   outside
order   story
systems
articulation
axis
verticality
section
body
wall

THE CENTRAL ACT OF SHAPING PLACE IS THE SEARCH FOR FORM. This search proceeds in concert with an evolving understanding of place. For us, it comprises analytic, intuitive, and sensate realms of exploration.

It is at times an ineffable, almost magical process. It is also highly iterative, with each new initiative informed by an evolving understanding of the numerous dimensions of the *genius loci*.

For centuries, architects have debated and proclaimed their understanding of the process of discovering appropriate forms. A look at some signal viewpoints illustrates the diversity of approaches.

The Ecole des Beaux Arts, established in 1863, insisted that students develop a "parti," typically a formal geometric diagram, as an armature for the full development of the building. This was conceived early on, and the success of the design lay in part in how clearly they could hew to the original diagram throughout their design process. "Parti" derives from the word "partisan," with the implication that students would become advocates for their original diagram.

"Form follows function," Louis Sullivan's canonical coinage, exemplifies the modern movement's tendency toward reductive formulations. While it is strictly true, if not tautological, it tends to validate the programmatic and analytic aspects of function and to slight, by omission, the cultural and experiential aspects of our environments.

Louis Kahn spoke of a process of crystallizing the formal diagram and then, as new information informs the process, dissecting and recrystalizing a more embracing form which subsumes greater complexity within a clear diagram. This resonates with the way in which scientists refer to the "elegance" of a solution: the more phenomena that can be explained by simplest theory, the more elegant.

7

Robert Venturi influentially reminded us of the "messy vitality" inherent in the understanding, accommodation, and responsiveness to the spatial and temporal layering of our world and cultures. His early manifesto *Complexity and Contradiction* renewed our perceptions of the breadth of form and language within which architects work with conviction and poetry.

At the same time, Charles Moore kept reminding us of the cultural diversity of the world, of the wisdom embedded within vernacular building, of the need to speak freely and without pious postures or ideologically inspired purity; all the while celebrating our shared human needs and aspirations.

With the backlash against the excesses of putative postmodernism and its trickle-down descendants of the 1980s, we have not only chastened ourselves, but we have ushered in a new self-limiting orthodoxy. The building as object is once again ascendant over buildings as places to inhabit. Context is seen as a minor relevance in an electronic environment. Societal and programmatic aspirations are often taken as low grade constraints beyond which the architect must quickly move.

We see the opportunity to renew and reassert the possibility of shaping places of individual character that are uniquely connected to their context, culture, and time. We embrace and explore the inherent tension between the desire for the "ideal" and the accommodation of the messiness of the real.

We find it critical to embrace the tension between the ideal and real, or the diagrammatic and the situational. This allows for both clarity of concept, and richness and specificity of experience and place.

These dualities are central to shaping places that are understandable and mysterious, archetypal and site-specific, conceptual and sensate.

8

Geometry and Order

The search for form is enhanced by the identification of a system that can be used to connect the physical and symbolic worlds. Geometry is a timeless tool for architects. Its etymology from the Greek for "measure of the world" (geo & metron: earth & measure), reinforces the power of the duality of the found physicality of the earth and the conceived abstraction of measure. This is central to our way of understanding and working. Such importance reverberates through time. As Peter Doyle, one of our mathematician clients at Dartmouth College told us, Aristotle's academy displayed the inscription "Let no one who is ignorant of geometry enter here."

Order is a much broader term than geometry. It encompasses such modes as numbers, sequences, structure, and systems. It too comprises both symbolic and physical schema, and thereby can help us to connect the experienced and imagined world to the material world.

Geometry and order have, since the earliest built form, embedded our cultural dimensions in our physical world.

The ancient Egyptians manifested a relatively static conception of the cosmos with their massive primary forms. The disposition of forms built in relation to the orientation of the Nile and the movement of the sun, connected them in life and death to the cycles of nature, reinforcing their reading of cosmic and diurnal cycles (fig. 7).

The Greeks built with a more complex and nuanced system. In their temples, geometric proportion, at both the building and detail scale, embodied the imputed characteristics of specific deities. Site planning developed with an ineffable sensitivity to topography, the perceived power of the forms of the earth, and great awareness of human movement through space and time. The dynamic complexity of their work is so rich that historians still debate both the prime motives and the nuances of the buildings (fig. 8).

9

As in all great architecture, the meaning embedded in the work is equally rich from the macro to micro, or from the regional to detailed scales, of conception and construction.

Geometry, order, and measure are not only generated from the abstract. An alternate and equally inspiring tradition involves the shaping of form through biomorphic references: forms analogized from nature. Two ancient traditions from vernacular architecture are the Trulli of the Abruzzi (fig.9) and the villages of West Africa (fig.10). Both manifest modular forms based on compound curvatures. In both cases the "system" is infinitely flexible, allowing for organic growth, variation in size, and construction using simple available and portable materials. The Trulli achieve exquisitely complex continuous surfaces from the artful stacking of simple flat stones. The African village uses mud and wattle shaped by the arc of the arm, smoothed and ornamented by hand. Both are reticulated to express both the individuality of family and function and the unity of village life. Both are well adapted to function and climate.

At the beginning of a new millennium, architects are using computers and theories of chance and chaos to find new formal languages unencumbered by the past. The sinuous surfaces derived from "blob theory," the fragments of fractal geometry, and the electrons of the age of communication ultimately must be translated into inhabited form. Whatever new formal languages we explore, their success will still reside in the shaping of places for human community and in making connections between us and the natural world.

Axes and Connections

If geometry and order can help us to give form to our understanding of place and culture, then axes and connections can help us shape the perception and experience of place.

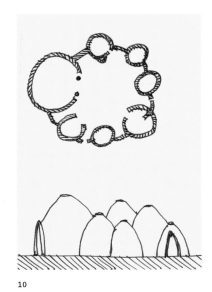

10

An axis simply connects two or more points or places. Connections comprise axes, but include as well an array of relationships such as physical, symbolic, kinesthetic, programmatic, and electronic modalities.

Both axes and connections operate in space and time, and both can be physical and symbolic. Our understanding of connections is increasingly dynamic in contemporary life. In the more stable worldview of the Egyptians, the axis of earth to sky connoted both the cycles of life and the relationship to the deities. The north-south axis of the Nile and the east-west axis of the sun completed the basic three-dimensional cosmology.

In a typical day we move through traditional axial connections of place—work/home, earth/sky—but we also experience the great circle of flight as the shortest distance between two cities. More abstractly we experience the daily electronic connections of data, which are networked as well as axial. Beyond such new ordinariness, we read of multi-dimensional time-space connections in evolving theories of physics. Even as this is written we hear new opportunities of connection: a scientist recently described "tubes" of relatively "frictionless" space where gravitational fields are balanced out and space travel can be accomplished with minimal energy; he imagines the uses of these "tubes" to help establish space stations and space hotels as part of our inevitable desire to explore and "build" in space.

We may be on the edge of explosive expansion of the scale in which we inhabit place. Yet our primal emotional, spiritual, and physical needs have changed minimally from the age of the earliest known builders. Physical and symbolic axes and connections continue to be powerful ways of understanding and shaping a set of meaningful relations to the built and natural world. They relate us to our past, strengthen our sense of the present, and project us imaginatively into the future.

11

Topography and Section

Architecture is a four-dimensional medium: space and time give meaning to each other. Unfortunately, much of the architecture and urbanism which we experience every day is conceived with minimal exploration of the third and fourth dimensions. While the two-dimensional manipulation of the plan in buildings, landscapes, and cities is the prime mover, it is in the vibrant three-dimensional development of architecture that we achieve full engagement of the mind and body. This seems so simple as to be axiomatic, but the pressures of the market, time, entropy, and perhaps impoverished aspirations often leave us with unleavened architecture

It has been said that the vertical axis is the dimension of aspiration in architecture. We need only recall our first experience of a Gothic cathedral, first sight of Rockefeller Center, or first ascent up a mountain to remember the sense of soaring in mind and body that such places engender.

The celestial dome, the dome of a building or our domicile, all have the same root: *domus* is Latin for house—*doma* in Greek. So whether we consider our shelter or our spirituality, we typically think of it as coming from above. Going down into the earth has had both connotations of fertility and birth (as in the Greek *tholos*) or of death and the afterlife. Traditionally, horizontal movement has related to diurnal activity and vertical to cosmic and lifecycles.

Yet with few exceptions we move through buildings and cities with little three-dimensional consciousness. Our office buildings are literally stacks of repetitive "floors." These are largely generated by the imperatives of the developer's "proforma," which works backwards from a desired R.O.I. (return on investment).
It is a self-reinforcing formula in which human "capital," as in human comfort, satisfaction, and aspirations are given little weight. Our houses and apartments are often dimensioned for the convenience and cost-effectiveness of the 8-foot stud.

12

Conversely, throughout history and across cultures we find both sacred and secular places where the shape of the land and spatial movement through buildings is celebrated.

Places that are memorable for their engagement of three dimensions can be thought of as primarily found or shaped. Those that are found involve recognition of and response to the natural topography of the earth. Places that are shaped involve the transformation of an imagined place into a place to be inhabited by body and mind.

Found forms involve an intimate dialogue between building and land. The Greek temple of Segesta in Sicily (fig. 11) presents an exquisite balance between the found and the shaped, with the building approximating the slope of the earth and sublimely framing near and distant landscapes.

Practically any Mediterranean hill-town takes its formal inspiration from topographic form. In cities like Urbino such sites were inspiration not only for the practicalities of the movement of goods, animals, and people, but also for the exuberant expression of the ways we can span, terrace, and build on shaped land. While the imperatives of contemporary planning and construction militate against such sensitive shaping, we certainly can find successful models for overcoming such institutional inertia. In many of his urban buildings, Giancarlo di Carlo has created exuberant contemporary responses to the land. As we move through his university buildings in Urbino (fig. 12), we are energized by our connection and rhythmic counterpoint to the land.

The topographic and sectional properties of a place are experienced in time. We find places with unique qualities and we engage them with our buildings; revealing the latent qualities, modifying the existing conditions, and shaping new dimensional experiences. The movement of our minds and bodies through the vertical dimension connects us to aspirational and transcendent meaning, reinforcing our sense of inhabiting places that link the earth and sky.

13

14

15

Dividing and Gathering: Wall and Pavilion

Dividing and gathering are two sides of the same phenomenon; like inside/outside, like space-time. In shaping, there is an impulse to differentiate the parts of a program or the places within a site, and then a corresponding desire to gather, to combine, to connect (fig. 13). In this kind of shaping we may be seeking to reflect our own bodies, which are after all deeply integrated constructions of remarkably disparate parts. We can also be inspired by other kinds of gatherings: the biotope, or the town (fig. 14).

Wonderful places have been created in this fashion, using the simplest of devices: the wall and the pavilion. The wall divides and defines, providing protection and control of a place that is separate from the world outside. The classical paradise garden—a walled space within which there is the opportunity to create order—is one of the earliest expressions of our need to separate, to distinguish, and to sanctify. The space within the enclosure can take on an extraordinary range of meanings and uses, from the commonly practical farmyard to the most sacred place of ritual.

The natural complement to the wall is the pavilion, which establishes a center. As an idea, the pavilion can be seen as just four columns and a roof, the roof differentiating and celebrating the space beneath. It provides a shelter we can go to and from which we can look out. The form is synonymous with house, and from the 19th-century theorist Laugier's famous log hut to the rediscovery of the aedicula by Charles Moore and Donlyn Lyndon in the early 1960s (fig. 15), it has inspired architects to find profound meaning in its centering, unitary form.

Louis Kahn's unbuilt plan for the de Vore House (fig. 16) makes elegant use of these two primary forms. The wall placed laterally through a grove of trees sets up an instant tension between the spaces on either side. This boundary is then brought to life by a gathering of pavilions that jostle along one side, with one pavilion jumping

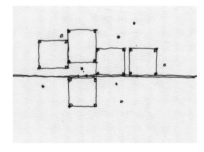

16

17

the wall to the other side. Even in the pure diagram, absent the further details of house planning—enclosing walls, windows, furniture—there is a kind of habitation taking place, a representation of community. For our purposes, this link between gathering forms and human community is essential.

For a kind of ultimate composition of the wall and pavilion, we like the classic Balinese Temple (fig. 17). The wall articulated by a split gateway encloses a compound for a gathering of pavilions: the bales, which are raised stone platforms covered by artfully made canopies of wood frame and thatch. The rich, multi-centered play of inside and outside, the collection of similar forms of varied heights and sizes, combined with the cosmological hierarchy of placement (mountain and sunrise orientations being more auspicious than directions toward seashore and sunset) are a beautiful model of house, temple, and community.

How might these primary forms apply to shaping community at a larger scale? Every city is essentially a composition of wall and house, the walls of enclosed blocks framing the network of streets, leading to significant freestanding houses, or their more public manifestations: churches, city halls, museums. The merging of these forms—the wall made of houses—continues to be compelling for contemporary architecture: we think of Ralph Erskine's Byker Wall housing in England and Kazuyo Sejima's Gifu Kitagata housing in Japan, both possibly inspired by Le Corbusier's famous wall housing proposal for Algiers.

Moore Lyndon Turnbull Whitaker's legendary Condominium 1 at the Sea Ranch is a splendid essay on wall and pavilion: 10 deceptively simple unit plans are assembled into a dense wall around two connected courtyards, and within each unit's enclosing walls a site is found for the famous four-poster/aedicula. Based on Charles Moore's Orinda House—a small pavilion containing two even smaller ones—the aedicula establishes a celebrated center, usually next to a stove or hearth, from

18

which to move out to the edges of the larger house. In terms of edges, the Condominium plan is almost symphonic in the ways it elaborates the conditions of inside and outside, and heightens the experience of habitation and shelter in the wild landscape of the Sea Ranch.

We are drawn to these simple forms as a basis for shaping because of their power to represent something essential about the world and our place in it (fig. 18). The wall demarcates and protects, just as the house/pavilion shelters and inhabits, and together as extensions of ourselves they may be gathered to establish place.

Sculpting by Addition and Subtraction

While houses and other familiar forms embrace habitation as protected and centered places, the body of a building can also have a different kind of totemic meaning—its visual impact or gestalt. Because so many building forms are repeated in our environment, we tend to notice this quality when presented with the exceptional: the power plant, the church, the train station, or more recently, the museum. Contemporary architecture seems preoccupied with such exceptional structures, seeking to present us with the pure sculptural impact of a made object, often a large one. In this effort, the hand and the processes of the sculptor are everywhere at work: assemblages, pure geometric shapes, found and re-used objects, twisted or "torqued" forms, and the appeal of surprising combinations of industrial components and materials.

As architects who look for meaning, and for deeper connections with our intrinsic need to inhabit, we are no less interested in the power of sculpted form. The approach most often taken is to apply the operations of the sculptor to simple or archetypal building forms, transforming them into a dynamic play of recognizable type and pure shape. Ideally, we would tap both the energy of the building as sculpture, and its iconic connection to culture, region, and place (fig. 19).

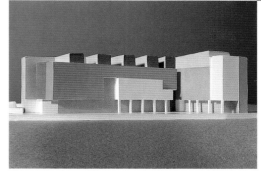

19   20

21

When it comes to this kind of shaping, our design process has always been physical and hands-on: simple models of paper or foam are prepared based on early sketches, and then reworked in a free-flow of iteration and restatement, using an x-acto knife and some double-stick tape. Forms are carved, pulled apart, combined, and recombined. In simplest terms, these are processes of addition—assembling discrete parts, stretching, repeating—and subtraction—carving out a singular form to create a more complex one (fig. 20).

In late classical architecture we have long admired the combining of pure forms by the 19th-century Berlin architect Ludwig Persius (fig. 21). Elemental gable-roofed pavilions are joined to open porches, cylindrical towers, and extended colonnades or pergolas, embracing the landscape, and combining the cultural spin of classicism with the modern invention of form. Tadao Ando's contemporary version of exactly the same formal process produces compositions of extreme beauty and serenity. Steven Holl, whose additive sculpting leads to a more provocative and contradictory whole, also maintains the duality of pure form and iconic connection to building type, as in his Hybrid Building for Seaside, Florida.

Perhaps the grandest example of design by subtraction is Haussmann's Boulevard Plan for Paris. The baroque idea of superimposing a super-scaled network of axial view corridors on an existing urban or landscape system provides a rich interplay of order and accident, of the large gesture and the local condition. The great carving of the broad boulevards enriches the building of the city, as each building in the plan has a special situation within the whole, a unique condition of intersecting geometries to solve.

The initial forms we like are simple, recognizable building forms, translated into rectilinear or geometric solids, walls, extended floor planes, and vertical elements like chimneys, towers, and sloping roofs, although we work to keep a tension

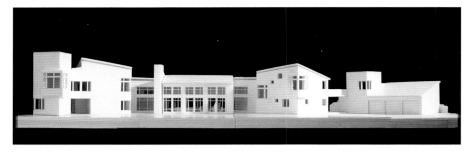

22

23

24

between the roof as a traditional element and the roof as an abstraction—a sliced-off cube or a sloping plane. Again, we want both meanings: the totemic and the iconic, the pure shape and the known, familiar form of building (fig. 22).

Inside/Outside

One of the most revealing expressions of place involves relations between inside and outside. Climate, obviously, but therefore culture and function, all conspire to influence how buildings and exterior places interact. Working in diverse settings, such as California and Sweden, we have been encouraged to think broadly and sometimes elaborately about how to interpret what is inside or outside, and how to establish the distinction between them. In terms of shaping, these thoughts most often lead to an enrichment of the plan or section of the building and/or its attendant outside.

This process of elaboration has its legitimate interest in the meanings of insides and outsides. While there is a general assumption that inside is shelter while outside is not, we look for a continuous and fine gradient of sheltering. Some of our buildings have been described as having rather casual, understated entries possibly because in our minds the moment of entry had already occurred within a court, or in stepping up onto a terrace, well before the front door was reached. Inside/outside is less a matter of shelter, and more a distinction of domains.

In the desire to explore and enhance the gradient of inside/outside, our plans tend to become complex and accommodating. Courts and gardens have equal standing with built interiors (fig. 23). Any space can become interior, relatively speaking, as building forms are shaped and adjusted around them. While this weaving of building and court is strongly Californian in inspiration, we continue to find that it can adapt to many climates. A house in a cold climate can benefit from a small court, protected from winds, where the winter sun can be gathered.

25

26

27

As much as we love the gradation from interior to exterior, we have not forgotten one of Charles Moore's favorite manipulations: the contrast and contradiction of inside and outside, ultimately the fairytale notion of "insides bigger than outsides." On the other hand, can inside and outside be truly simultaneous? Norman Foster's glass dome over the Reichstag in Berlin provides a unique inside/outside experience. Inside the dome we are still not in the building, but in an open rooftop pavilion devoted most of all to looking out, with a dizzying glimpse of the parliament hall below. Climbing the ramp, we float in a crystalline bubble that gathers all the city around into a classic panorama (fig. 24).

At a more intimate scale, the shaping of inside and out links the specifics of context to the deeper needs of habitation. Certain forms accomplish this kind of joinery so well that we keep returning to them: bay windows, usually with a seat, and porches and small rooms that emerge through the roof to look out and beyond (fig. 25). Just as Frank Lloyd Wright was keen on the center—every house has a hearth under a low canopy with a spreading, horizontal view from the center out—we are excited by the possibilities of habitation at the boundary, at the transition, where we can be both places at once (fig. 26).

This simultaneous experience of inside/outside is exponentially increased by the visual connection, the view. Approaching the building, we see a tower room or an attic space with a high dormer window, and want to go there at once, knowing how a small room can be forever linked by its view to a grand and distant landscape (fig. 27).

Narrative and Metaphor

As an ordering principle, narrative structure can offer a way of shaping that enhances our understanding of habitation in a particular place. Fundamentally different from ordering techniques based on geometric form, repetition, or simple hierarchy, the shaping of narrative appropriates other strategies in a unique

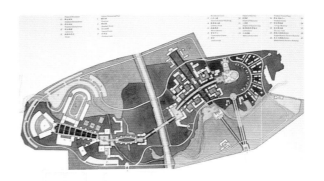

28

sequence, based on special insights, needs, and desires. If shaping by geometry offers up a crystal, narrative assembles a protein. Narrative shaping incorporates the complexities of experience, surprise, memory, anticipation, and choice (fig. 28).

Narrative forms are inherently metaphoric in that we are presented with a structure that, whatever its own qualities, is also about something else. The narrative shaping of a house—in which we approach, arrive, choose, discover, return, repose, recall—is almost certainly about the character of the site, or at least the site in conjunction with our clients' vision of how to live there. The complex meanings that are folded into our desire to live in a special way in a particular place may be celebrated through metaphor.

People understand narrative shaping intuitively, because in addition to having great spatial cognition and memory, we are a species of storytellers. As a way to understand our place in nature—the enormous reality of life, the smaller role of our species as part of a grand evolutionary sequence, and the therefore highly relative scale of our own lives—we look to the myth, the story, as the truest form that represents the meaning of each individual life, linking our discrete time in the world to something larger. Narratives in architecture can also take on mythic proportions: grand sequences like the rooms of the Pergamon Museum in Berlin, or urban passages like Unter den Linden and its axial extension through Brandenburg Gate and the Tiergarten, linking civic, monumental places and landscape.

The structural form for a narrative sequence can be as simple as an axis or spine, which may then be bent, broken, and reconnected, or split—or not. Wilshire Boulevard in Los Angeles is miles long and straight, except for one or two wiggles and bends; like a section line through the city, it leads forward and backward in time as it cuts across neighborhoods and districts from this or that decade—a decade being for Angelenos almost like geologic time. Partly due to scale, Los Angeles rewards the

29

automobile tour: the sensuous weaving of Sunset Boulevard, for example, suddenly bursting into the "strip" where buildings of all ages and types vie with billboards to tell a popular story.

Narrative can be quietly reflective and nuanced, as is the Louisiana Museum (fig. 29) outside Copenhagen, which presents a seemingly spontaneous movement between distinct parts, each taking a slightly different attitude relative to the landscape, all loosely connected around a beautiful garden. Except for the older house at the entrance, no piece of the composition quite seems like a building, but each is a condition of (partial) enclosure, orientation, light, elevation, and view. Here we see how profoundly interdependent are the parts of a narrative shaping, and in the almost accidental passage from one to the next, how our sense of expectation is heightened and rewarded.

Tod Williams and Billie Tsien's Neurosciences Institute in La Jolla, California uses this kind of narrative shaping to explore the poetics of materials and place on its hillside site. Moving up the hill between what are not so much buildings as elements of building, one is brought to particular moments that are about some pure quality: reflectivity, the hinging of a wall, the patterns of a wooden screen, the peculiar sheen of a concrete surface, and for architects, the dumb urge to find out where they got that stone! One slips inside and out without quite realizing it, and while the overall composition is both moving and memorable, the exact arrangement remains elusive.

Narrative shaping, perhaps more than any other, speaks to the subtlety and complexity of habitation and experience, with important allusions to our native capacity for storytelling and myth making.

Clarice Smith Performing Arts Center
University of Maryland, College Park, Maryland

The Performing Arts Center evolved as an articulated academic village with a rich multiplicity of scales, paths, and environments. It is unique in its programmatic aspirations. Academic departments for music, theater, and dance are combined with an array of practice and performance venues and an arts library, in a mix that balances the needs and domains of departments, of the campus, and of the region. A key design challenge was to create departmental identities that could co-exist with the large-scale reading of the project as a campus and regional cultural center. With over 300,000 square feet, the Clarice Smith Performing Arts Center takes its place on the periphery of the campus, flanked by massive parking areas, the stadium, and high-rise student housing.

A Campus Within a Campus
The early planning for the Center established the concept of a series of departmental courtyards to enhance individual identity and domain. Each of these is oriented along one of the adjacent campus axes. At the confluence of these domains, a dominant axis leads from a public entry plaza, flanked by the arts library, through an interior street and out to a naturally sloped amphitheater.

Rethinking Campus Language
The building developed formally as an assemblage of Platonic forms, that reflects the complexity and hierarchy of internal ritual and function. This expression of taut skinned, volumetrically clear solids became a primary way of harmonizing a modern formal language with the existing Georgian campus architecture. The language of white windows and porches was reinterpreted as a family of white metal light scoops or lanterns, and a series of simple metal porches and bays.

The forms are quiet toward the periphery where simple porches and stair towers reinforce entry. The gathering of performance spaces builds up to the large form of the major concert hall. For economy most forms derive from cubic geometry with flat or shaped roofs for iconic and programmatic reasons. Courtyards, allées, and passages are shaped as positively configured open spaces; vessels for movement and habitation.

Gathering Halls
Along the "main street" of the complex, each of seven major performance venues has a presence. Each venue is conceived as a uniquely shaped object or pavilion with individual entry porticos. The group becomes a family of forms connected and gathered by stairs, walls, and balconies, which animate the path. Entries to a café, garden, library, and exhibition space further enliven this central armature to create a multidimensional social and cultural venue. Here a diverse community interacts in serendipitous or programmed gatherings.

Multi-Sensory Shaping
Our most powerful inspirations for these forms were light and sound.

A series of lanterns, clerestories, and bays illuminate practice spaces, performance halls, and paths. Daylight is typically brought in high, and bounced through expressed structure, finally to wash the walls in soft and shifting light. Since the building has opened, this changing, complex environment has become a powerful magnet for social and academic interaction. At night, the syncopated reading of the lanterns provides a beguiling intimation of the creative flux within.

>>>>

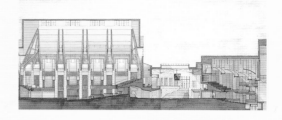

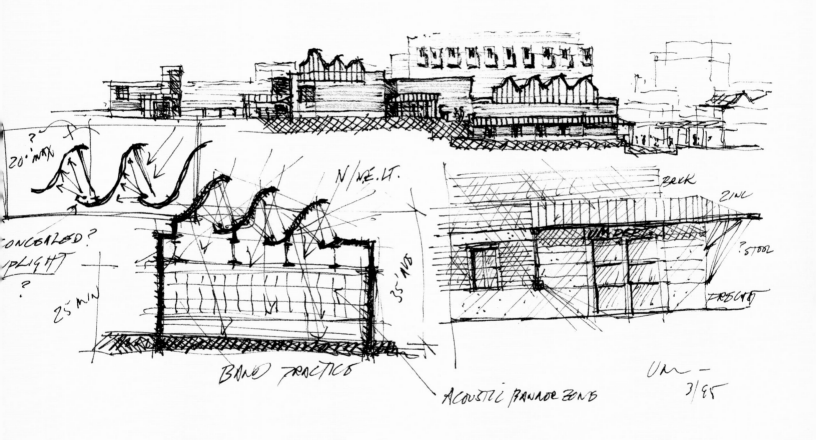

Light is a strong determinant of form.

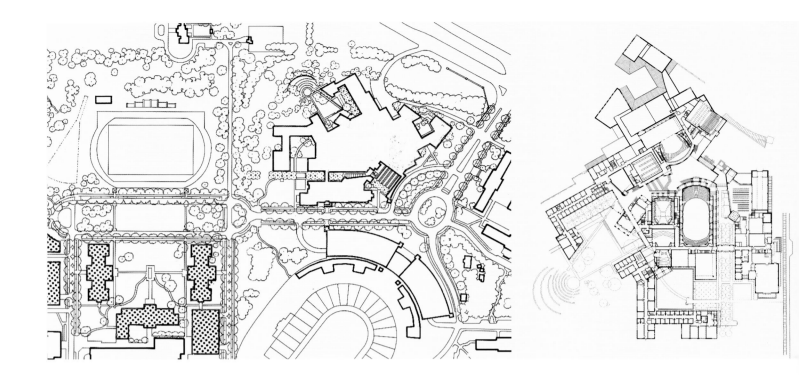

Sound was both a powerful and a subtle influence: volumes and proportions of spaces established acoustic qualities, which were further enhanced by material choices.

Sight and sound were also critical ways of shaping the major halls. Working with our clients, Theater Projects and Larry Kirkegaard (acoustics), we explored the unique characters that express the essential possibilities of each space.

· The dance theater is muscular and direct in both shape and structure, yet daylight and color give it a lively and unpredictable quality.

· The 650-seat theater is extraordinarily intimate, richly detailed, and colored in warm dark woods and colors that embrace the audience yet focus on the performers.

· The recital hall is shaped to be comforting and elegant; flexible enough to allow for small events, but ceremonial enough to honor the accomplishments of students in performance.

· The steeply pitched roofs and expressed structure of the 1150-seat concert hall produce a bold, tectonic, and inspirational space. In section this hall is shaped both for acoustic reflections and for the diffusion of light. Light enters through clerestory bays and is softened through layered walls, which also support audience and technical balconies. In plan, the house is shaped to enhance the close communal experience of music and to allow for a sense of intimacy, whether partly or fully occupied. This is, in the end, an instrument for sound, light, meditation, and community.

Towers scoop light into studios as they dance
across the landscape.

Along the "main street" of the complex, each of seven major
performance venues has a presence. The group becomes a family of
forms connected and gathered by stairs, walls and balconies,
which animate the path.

The concert hall seats 1150 with unusual intimacy.

>>>>

The dance theater is muscular and direct in
both shape and structure.

The building developed formally an as an assemblage of Platonic forms, that express the complexity and hierarchy of internal ritual and function.

Joseph & Alma Gildehorn Recital Hall: shaped
to be comfortable, elegant, and ceremonial.

Daylight is brought in high and bounced
through expressed structure.

Shmuger/Hamagami House
Pacific Palisades, California

Our clients for this house are a young energetic family who hoped to maximize both delight and economy. They sought the playfulness and sensuousness of curved forms both because of the wife's background as a modern dancer and for their energetic young sons.

A curving spine organizes and shapes the house.

The Dancing House
The house evolved as a metaphor for both body and movement. A curving spine organizes and animates the house. Discreet yet connected, family spaces are arrayed along the spine on the ground level. They reach out to the landscape like limbs, defining and embracing intimate outdoor spaces.

Upstairs, the spine connects children's rooms to the master bedroom. Here the spine is shaped as a family seating area with benches and shelves carved into its form. At one end, a small "pocket study" perches over the entry below. A second study sits higher with views to distant landscapes.

Movement throughout the house is suggested but not constricted by the shaping of interior volumes, allowing for a diversity of types of movement and discovery. The house is experienced both as a body containing social domains and as a form, which encourages our own bodies to move dynamically through space.

The plan of the house is contained within the narrow, buildable portion of a very steep lot. The house is composed vertically to optimize physical and visual connections to the slopes of the near and distant landscape. The back garden, shaped by the confluence of hillside and house, links through the central gallery of the house to a front terrace garden, which spills down in layers from informal lawn to native hillside plantings. The spine of the house links the entry court through the gallery, on to an intimate living room, and is completed by a quiet shaded garden, a contemplative and cerebral termination of the house as body.

The Sculpted Shed
To achieve a design that could support a rich array of movement and experience on a strict budget, we adopted a rigorous strategy. We began with simply shaped, easily built pitched roof volumes. These were carved from the outside to create forms that engage the landscape and the natural light. Inside, the more complex curved and angled geometries were developed to enhance movement and domain. The simpler, exterior forms are easy to construct and less expensive to make weatherproof. The more complex forms, sculpted elements within the sheltering shed, animate the life of the family.

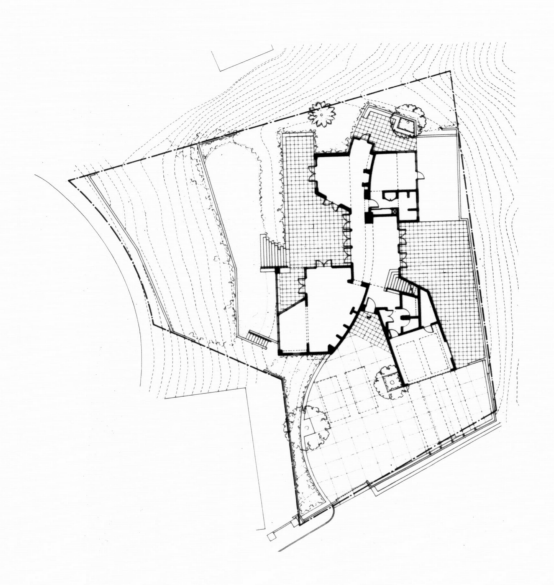

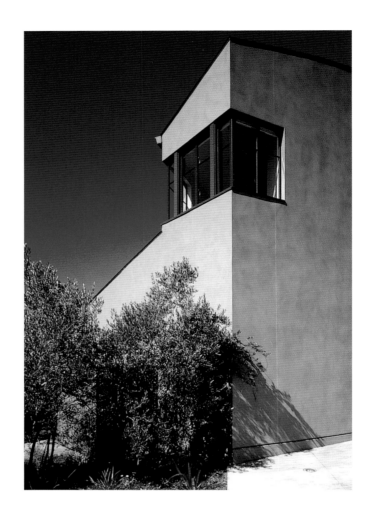

We began with simply shaped, easily built pitched roof volumes. These were carved from the outside to create forms that engage the landscape and the natural light.

Light and movement animate the house.

The spine of the house links the entry court,
through the gallery, to an intimate living room.
<<<<

United States Courthouse and Federal Building
Fresno, California

The courthouse is a classic building type, deeply associated with American history, place, and culture. Contemporary courthouses have evolved into a new type, with altogether different problems of scale, organization, security, and functional complexity–yet at their core, the original courtroom can still be found, with its original sense of decorum and drama. The challenge of modern courthouse design is to find appropriate expression for the building as a representation of the civic institution of the law, and for the Federal Courthouse, as a symbol of the Federal Government in a local place. In terms of place, Fresno's downtown scores famously low on the context and character scale. The true context of the Courthouse, appropriate to its regional function, is the agricultural landscape surrounding the city–California's great Central Valley.

Iconic Shaping

Fresno's new courthouse is large–a result of its program and the two-story height of the typical courthouse floor–and sufficiently imposing by its sheer mass that we sought ways to divide, articulate, open up, and lighten the form into numerous parts. This complexity, which is also inherent in the program, is then reunified by shaping. The shaping of the courthouse draws on the power of familiar local monuments–the nearby Sierra Nevadas. The mass is folded into an L of two slowly colliding volumes, with solid shoulders and sloping tops. At the apex, a grand loggia frames views over Fresno's green suburbs, the tree plantations of the Valley, and the snow-capped peaks.

Porch and Panorama

Embracing landscape qualities as varied as the region's mountain streams, oak-dotted foothills, and sweeping agricultural plains, the site design of the courthouse is all about place. The L-shape of the building frames a large public garden, designed by Pamela Burton as a tableau to be seen from the lobby, a tall glassy porch. Few courthouse lobbies offer this kind of continuous experience of landscape: one enters along a walk tangent to the garden, turns through a vestibule, and crossing the lobby looks back at the outdoor com-

position, a kind of living diorama. Artists Anna Valentina Murch and Doug Hollis have heightened the experience by bringing thematic landscape elements–rocks from their stream-bed fountain, a well, and an orange tree–into the lobby itself. The historic role that 19th-century artists performed in presenting the landscape of the American West to a new nation is redoubled–the art *is* the landscape.

Galleries of Light and Litigation

From the lobby garden, courthouse visitors are brought to elevators serving stacks of glassy galleries poised over the courtyard, looking back to the city. As settings for pre-trial activity the galleries are not insignificant–we imagine deals, strategies, and moments of truth that have ultimate importance in the individual and collective lives of the people. The glass walls of the galleries are gently bowed, playing against the solid, textured concrete walls of the building and giving a subtle sense of pressure–the flow of human activity and destiny held within the solid frame of the law.

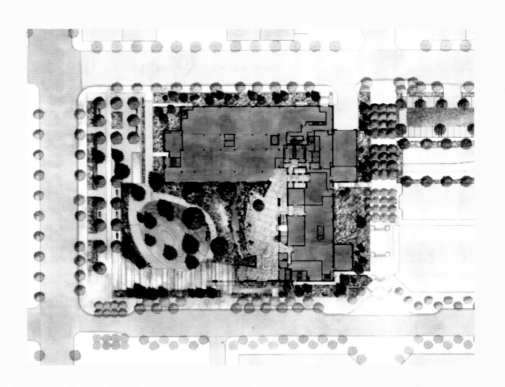

The courthouse mass is folded into an L of two
slowly colliding volumes, with solid shoulders
and sloping tops, framing a civic garden.

At the apex, a grand loggia frames views over
Fresno's green suburbs, the tree plantations of
the valley, and the snow-capped peaks of the
nearby Sierra Nevadas.

Santa Monica Main Library
Santa Monica, California

Santa Monica is almost perfect: a mild but sunny climate, broad beaches, dramatic bluffs, boulevards lined with palms, a progressive city council, and a beach town atmosphere and scale—very few buildings are more than four stories—that clearly distinguishes this prosperous little community from the surrounding city of Los Angeles. Santa Monica's urban grid marches steadily up to the bluffs and the beach, with a single street, Colorado Avenue, projecting out into the Pacific on the deck of the old pier. With its small town character, this is a place in which every new building has an impact.

In a recent poll, the city's most popular institution was its Main Library, and the design of the new library has been closely attended by city officials and the public. The program is moderate in size, but great in ambition. Our clients wanted no less than a model of a 21st-century

city library: friendly and service-oriented, flexible, with the latest in information systems, a certified LEED silver rating for sustainability, abundant below-grade parking, and a café that would allow the facility to become "the living room of the city."

The site occupies half a downtown city block, seven blocks from the beach, with a glimpse of the water looking south down Santa Monica Boulevard. The area is generous for the Library program, which has allowed for flexible planning and room to expand. From the outset, design was guided by the goals of community and placemaking, not all of which were consistent with conventional wisdom for library planning.

Converging and Gathering
Despite the classic library dictum of a single guarded entrance, it is important to connect the library as closely as possible to its surrounding edges. Pedestrians are brought in from all the adjacent streets to enter the building at a gathering place near the center of the block. Entrances at either end of a wide gallery bring the public to a single information and circulation area.

Garden for Reflection and Fantasy
Santa Monica is a green city, with a famed collection of street trees and

numerous parks. In keeping with this quality, interiors are interspersed with gardens—the partly enclosed gardens enrich the street edges as well as light the interiors. At the center of the whole is a large garden court, with controlled access permitting the space to be used by readers. A small café animates the court and provides a destination. Artist Carl Cheng has introduced a broad, circular canopy that intersects the glassy corner of the café. Using open steel trellis-work, water-filled glass "lenses," and a delicate water curtain, the canopy elicits a dreamy space filled with watery reflections and filtered light: an evocation of the undersea world of Santa Monica Bay. With a planting palette of cool colors and picaresque forms, Pamela Burton's garden design completes the picturesque allusion.

>>>>

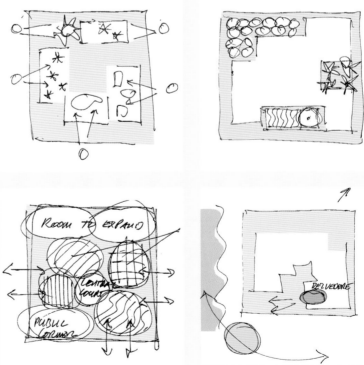

The inverted roof form, a classic Roman-style impluvium, is projected over a grand entry porch on Santa Monica Boulevard.

Opening and Invitation

Reader spaces within the Library are visible from the street. The principal elevation along Santa Monica Boulevard presents a long, narrow, two-story reading room with a continuous floor-to-ceiling window. At the base of the window, banquette seating under a low canopy creates an intimate edge poised slightly above the sidewalk. Other spaces feature bay windows at upper levels, inviting passersby to see the activities within.

Inverted Roof

The program works best in a two-story scheme—a challenge in creating the kind of scale that would make a civic focal point within the Library's commercial/residential district. The inverted roof form, a classic Roman-style impluvium, makes the highest part of the building out at the street edge, sloping gently down into the central garden. The roof slope is expressed at the interior, giving variety and character to the large open spaces of the second floor Reference Library. High windows with sun controls bring natural light deeply into the spaces. The roof also collects rainwater for the library's underground cisterns, just like a Roman villa.

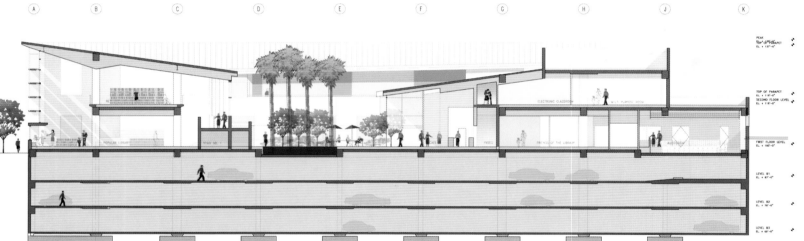

At the center of the whole, a large garden court with a café provides a destination.

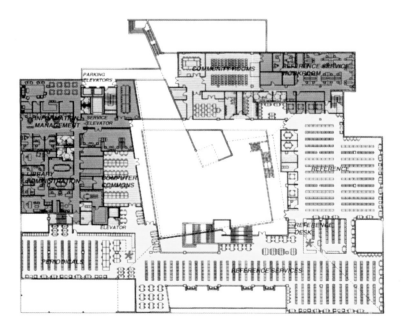

Partly enclosed gardens enrich the street
edges as well as light the interiors.

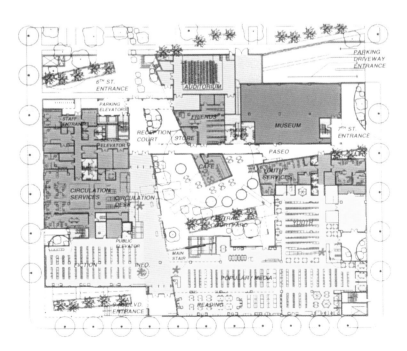

Beijing Century Center
Beijing, People's Republic of China

Our passion to discover modern China, and to seek its opportunities, led us into a design competition for this commercial development, located on a prominent Third Ring site in Beijing's diplomatic quarter. The program of office towers and large hotel is one that is repeated throughout the city, with mediocre results stemming from the developers' common vision of Beijing as a purely international or "world" city, based exclusively on imported design. To their credit, most builders eschew trite variations on pagoda roofs, but we still hoped for some meaningful connection to the dense cultural history of China.

Art into Planning
In our previous work in the region—the master plan of Dong-Hwa National University campus in Taiwan, and our unselected competition bid for the Shanghai Grand Theater—we searched for insight not in architecture per se, but in art and landscape design. The plan of Dong-Hwa, for example, was inspired by a scroll painting depicting at one point a small village and a nearby temple complex joined by bridges across a bend in the river. The everyday quality of the village and the auspicious nature of the temple are beautifully conveyed, and led us to a more overt sense of hierarchy and distinction between academic and residential areas of the campus plan.

Rock into Tower
For the Beijing project, the commercial program and planning limits suggested two towers and the hotel, which other competitors treated as a third tower, producing very similar designs. We had been impressed with the gnarled, columnar rocks—some nearly 20 feet tall— that we saw in gardens in the Forbidden City. Like the vertiginous mini-mountains of Qui Lin in southern China, these grotesque forms seem uniquely Chinese, and a fine metaphor for a large-scale urban form. As the modeling of the office buildings proceeded, these shapes were abstracted in a nearly symmetrical

pairing of the towers into a single monumental form, whose gently bowed sides featured massive projecting volumes. At the cross-axis of the split tower a three-story bridge links the offices to the hotel.

Hotel into Zocalo
The urban benefit of the hotel is the public space it offers. Hotels throughout Asia provide extremely popular gathering places, for the public as well as the guests, and typically have a rich program of restaurants, entertainment, and shops. Thinking of Beijing's miserable climate—hot and humid for half the year and dry, dusty, and bitterly cold the other half—we organized the hotel as a midrise, with room floors wrapping three sides of a grand atrium—an acclimatized public square where the air is always clean. The relatively low volume of the hotel provides a yin-yang companion for the towers, strengthening the urban composition into two complementary forms set in a small urban park.

The mid-rise hotel wraps a grand atrium—a
social heart with a tempered environment.

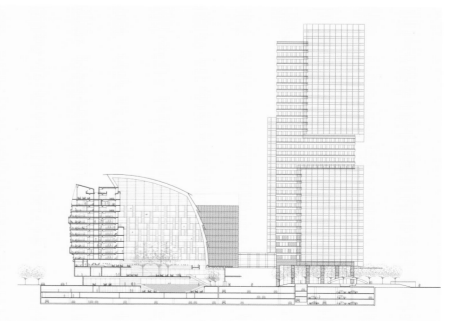

Paired towers inspired by garden stones.

United States Air Force Memorial Competition
Arlington, Virginia

In 2002, the United States Air Force Foundation invited four firms to participate in a competition for concepts for a new Air Force Memorial at a bluff-top site adjacent to Arlington Cemetery.

Memory and Meditation
Our design evolved as a dynamically shaped place in which site topography begins and ends a narrative experience. The built structure engages the body and spirit in a choreography of intimate and grand places. It is a passage from earth to sky and back, a meditation on the past, a kinesthetic experience in the present, and a speculation on the future.

The array of environments and experiences, which are shaped by the architecture, evokes the ethos and mission of the Air Force. As such, it celebrates the individual and collective experience, contributions, and aspirations.

The experience of the memorial begins with a gently sloped "runway" whose trajectory surrounds the dome and then escapes the atmosphere to soar beyond. The dome springs from the earth at the five points of a star. It is formed by the intersection of great circles, which combine to frame key views to adjacent monuments and to the sky and space beyond.

Connecting Earth and Sky
At the top of the dome, the great circles align to form an oculus: a window that connects us to the dynamic experience of space. The gently sloped base of the dome evokes both the land and water of earth, dynamically reflecting the shapes of the dome and the movement of the sun and clouds.

The entire site is shaped as a sequence of places of memory, reverence, and celebration.

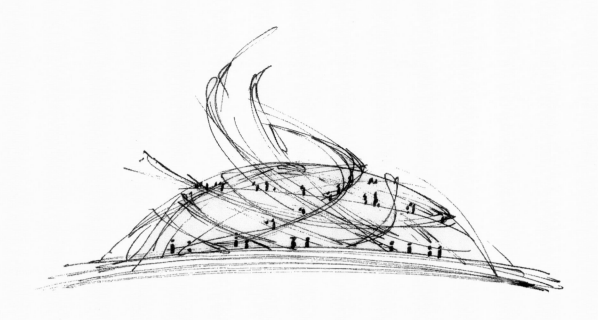

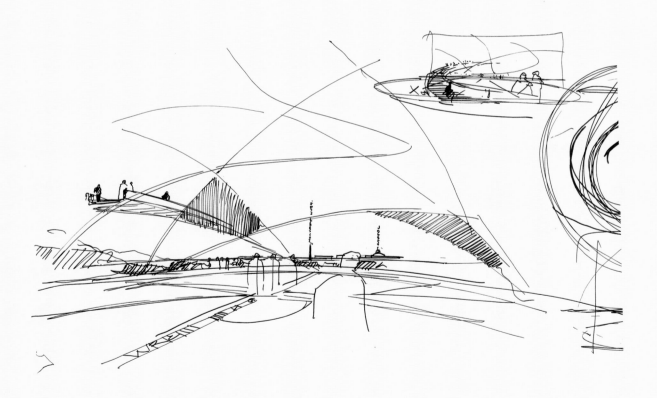

Trajectories trace earthly movement, then
soar beyond.

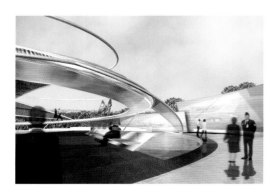

Great circles align to form an oculus.

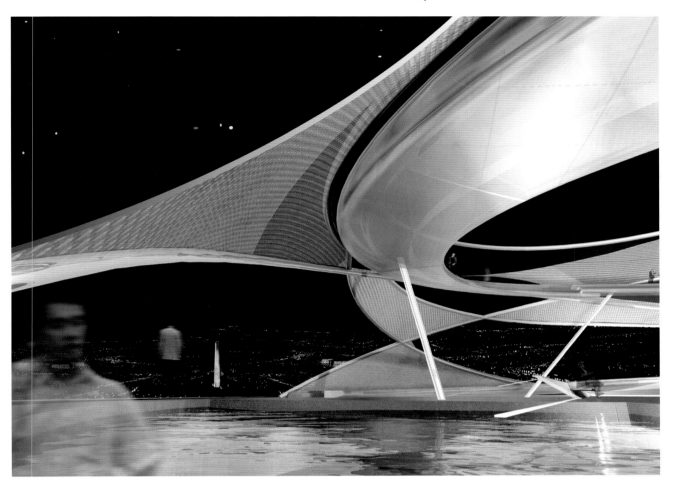

The structure forms places for movement and reflection.

Potatisåkern Housing
Malmö, Sweden

The central, historic part of Malmö and its neighboring university town, Lund, have the visual richness, scale, and tireless appeal of places built by accumulation: narrow streets open unexpectedly onto cobblestone squares and green parks. Small civic buildings, market halls, and train stations focus community activity and add their special character as building types. The town fabric of predominately two- to four-story buildings are made of brick, with tile or metal roofs, and together with the occasional white or colored plaster wall, and the constantly shifting surfaces and details, the whole adds up to a stirring visual treat. In Malmö the scale is more urban, with the added dimension of a variety of waterfronts and edges—a Baltic town that is under-appreciated only because it is outdone by Copenhagen across the water.

The site of Potatisåkern, the eponymous potato field, looks across a waterfront park toward the Öresund and Copenhagen, and is surrounded by a gentle green district that includes some of Malmö's finest old villas. It is prime real estate—so prime that after years of planning attempts by public and private agencies, no development was quite good enough. In the mid-1980s a consortium of the city's four largest developers decided to seek outside help to break the stalemate.

The Luxury of Choice
From our point of view we could say with only slight exaggeration that the project began in 1986 with a 10-minute phone call, was conceived in about 40 minutes, and built in sixteen years. During that time the program evolved from its original goal of giving new life and form to classic Swedish social housing, and became market rate rental housing with a luxury standard. For MKB, Malmö's public housing company, the project became a vehicle for a new vision of housing driven not by standardization, but by quality and choice.

Axis and Crescent
The shaping of Potatisåkern begins with a form for its waterfront edge—a Bath-inspired crescent with a central gap to open the water view to the deep rectangle of the site. From the crescent an axis is drawn through to a neighborhood landmark, the German Church at the back of the site. This central axis is crossed by other visual axes drawn from surrounding streets.

>>>>

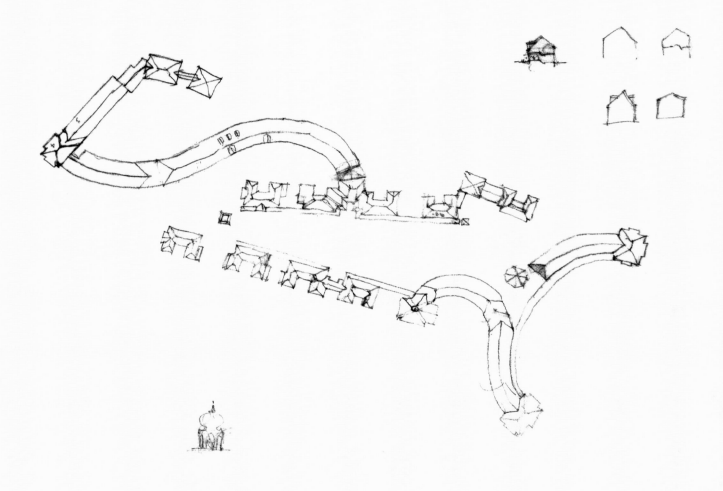

Potatisåkern's plan marries axial and serpentine geometries.

The Crescent embraces a grassy terrace looking
out to the Öresund

Villa and Snake

Two complementary building forms, long curvilinear wall-buildings and singular houses or villas, are organized to shape landscape places along the axis and crescent. The gentle meander of the wall-buildings—the "crescent" and the "snake"—mediates their scale as they wind in and out of view. The villas form chorus lines that splay to either side of a grand central lawn, their repeated forms and varied colors and details suggesting an orderly community. These same building types were a feature of our housing at Berlin's Tegel harbor, but at Potåtisakern their scale was increased considerably, and the whole succeeds largely because color, detail, and character are strong enough.

Inhabiting the Rooftops

The making and materials draw directly from the rich context of Malmö and Lund with special attention to the edges of ground and sky. The brick walls of the crescent and snake are completed by zinc paneling at the upper floors and roof, where the architecture merges with the changing atmosphere. In some places, long roof terraces have glassy canopies, and lantern-rooms rise up for distant views. The villas are even more playful: their large roofs come in a variety of materials and colors, sporting chimneys, urns, clerestory windows, and dormers to warm up the gray winter skies with an active silhouette. The ochre brick walls of the snake and crescent set a textured background for the brilliantly colored plaster shapes of the villas.

Garden Geometries

Building and landscape are intertwined, and a varied repertoire of garden forms emerges from the strong shaping of the plan. The Crescent Terrace offers a raised lawn with a view toward the sea; the adjacent Sun-dial Court, almost always in shadow, is granite-paved with huge roman numerals lit sequentially by low spotlights. The trapezoid of the Central Lawn is attended by a series of square gardens and play areas between the villas, and climbs gently to a raised, circular disc—a compass of polished stone, from which axial walks radiate. At the far end of the axis, the last villa and the snake converge and then open out to frame Sailor's Gate, a trumpet-shaped entry place opposite the German Church. In this little square, a play structure of stone and bronze hints at a Viking boat— a detail inspired by the model ships that hang in the foyers of churches all over southern Sweden.

Sailor's Gate draws the great curves down to neighborhood scale.　　　　>>>>

Inhabited roofs create a distinct domain.

A pergola holds the Crescent's arc as the
buildings pull away.

Materials meet at various levels—brick from
ground up and zinc from the sky down.

United States Embassy
Berlin, Germany

In 2003 we have prepared further designs for the new American Embassy in Berlin, modifying our original competition-winning scheme from 1996 to meet new security and site conditions. We have also taken advantage of the intervening years by making the scale and character of the Embassy more responsive to a dramatically transformed context, which now includes the completed government center, the remodeled Reichstag with Norman Foster's legendary dome, and a new building next door by Frank Gehry. These moments of civic pride and modern design will be further complemented by the immense Monument to the Murdered Jews of Europe, just to the south of the Embassy site, and crowned by the cleaned and restored Brandenburg Gate, which brightly anchors the center of this grand civic district.

Public/Private
Embassies are unique in their dialectic pairing of highly public representation and extraordinary privacy and security requirements. The Berlin Embassy expresses the essential fact of a secure compound using the courtyard building type, a classic form in European cities. The stone wall exterior with its regular grid of punched windows is activated by a set of larger sculptural openings with metal and glass volumes that are carved into, set on top of, or placed just outside of the walls.

Sculpting Light
On Pariser Platz the simple stone façade is dramatically split to form an entry with a cylindrical court that provides the main lobby. Over the lobby a "wave" of steel and glass canopy projects out like a wing protecting the entry. The entry itself is light and glassy between the stone walls, and carefully scaled to welcome individuals as well as groups. The carved opening brings a wash of light into an otherwise shadowy northwest wall, and lights the flag as it swoops out at a jaunty angle over the sidewalk.

Rustic Center
Inside the walls is a multilevel set of courtyard gardens with a house of hospitality in the middle—the Lodge. This community focal point provides dining,

meeting, and lounge spaces for events and daily activities, bringing the Embassy staff together in a place of collegiality. The parti for the Lodge features a pair of massive stone chimneys. Their form and texture establish a rustic central hearth, crisscrossed overhead by angular roof planes and clerestory windows. Evergreen trees in the lower garden frame the terrace for gatherings in front of the Lodge, while a backyard garden combines flowering deciduous trees, a small lawn, and patio with a barbeque for holiday parties.

State House Lantern
Opposite the Tiergarten the Embassy rooftop is mounted by a penthouse, a house of State whose focal point is the glassy conference room of the Lantern. Using only soft interior lighting at night, the Lantern joins both the Reichstag's dome and the Quadriga sculpture on the Brandenburg Gate, as part of the civic district's collection of skyline landmarks. The view from the Lantern has been carefully composed to show the Quadriga as it seems to ride across the Embassy's rooftop parterre garden of native American grasses.

>>>>

On Pariser Platz the simple stone façade is dramatically

split to form an entry with a cylindrical court.

The sculpted entry court brings a wedge of
light onto Pariser Platz.

Garden Overlay

Increased setbacks along two principal
frontages, Behrenstrasse and Ebertstrasse, prompted a renewed interest in
urban landscape. Treating the bird's-eye
view of the site as a "fifth elevation" to
be designed by Laurie Olin and Susan
Weiler as a whole, the landscape design
embraces virtually every horizontal surface. From the geometry of the parterre
garden along Ebertstrasse, which is
extended to the Ambassador's Roof Garden, then to green roofs planted with
carpets of sedum, and down the walls
and into the courtyards, landscape materials inspired by places of the American
continent give the Embassy a green narrative, and link the site to the grand
context of the Tiergarten.

The lodge provides a place of community and
hospitality for embassy staff and visitors.

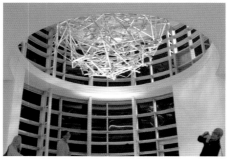

Rooftop sculpture and shifting planes along
Ebert Strasse.   >>>>

144

Baas/Walrod House
The Sea Ranch, California

This house composes a set of elemental forms to explore the latent complexities of its setting at the brow of the hill. The seam between meadow and forest is celebrated by the house as a linear extrusion which mediates this transition. On the south a continuous porch enfronts the ocean view. On the north it is shaped to complete an implied apsidal space made by the nearby redwoods. The resulting space has an archetypal reference: part sacred grove, part amphitheater.

Entry proceeds from a parking court through a thick "servant" wall and then through the portal between house and studio. This covered space frames views south to the ocean and north to the forest, and celebrates the movement and interaction between meadow and forest.

Loft and Light
The main living space is conceived as one great loft with sleeping, bathing, and cooking areas experienced within communicating bays. The hearth anchors the space and marks the boundary between the protected interior and the primal grove. North light is scooped in through high monitors.

Intimate and Particular
The study and guest areas fit compactly into the smaller wing, linked by porch and roof. Here, a set of intimate and highly particularized spaces includes study, bath, and sleeping bay on the first level, connected by a winding stair to a study, tatami bay, and sleeping bay upstairs. All of this occurs within a 20 x 20 foot square plan and contrasts tightly packed places with the open loft of the partner space.

The building is crafted in expressed post and beam. A stained concrete floor and stained wooden walls add subtle colors which link to the landscape.

Like its landscape, this modest house is by turns serene and bold, expansive and intimate, refined and rugged.

The building is shaped to engage the
landscape and topography.

The seam between meadow and forest is celebrated by the house as a linear extrusion which mediates this transition.

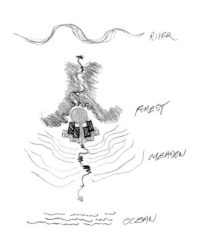

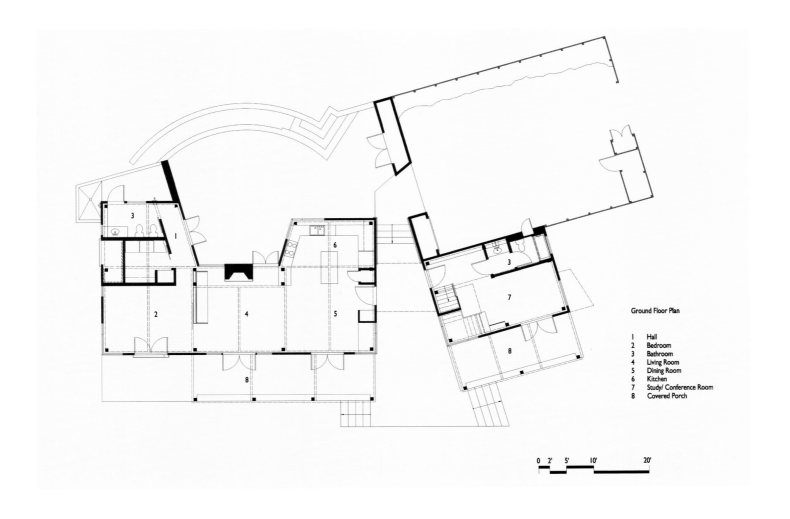

Ground Floor Plan

1 Hall
2 Bedroom
3 Bathroom
4 Living Room
5 Dining Room
6 Kitchen
7 Study/ Conference Room
8 Covered Porch

0 2' 5' 10' 20'

A thick "servant" wall mediates between
parking and forested courtyard.   >>>>

Materials are crafted with a direct expression.

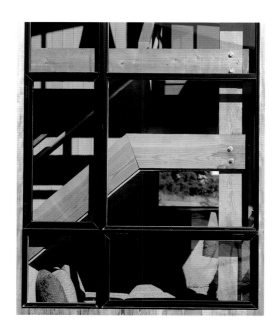

Intimate bays closely fit the body and connect to the land.

The House at Sea Ranch

Jacquelyn Bass

I FIRST SAW THE SEA RANCH ON AUGUST 10, 1985. That was the year Charles Moore's Hood Museum of Art opened at Dartmouth College, where I was director. On a California college tour with my son, I insisted we visit The Sea Ranch so I could see Moore's famous condominium there. We drove all the way from San Francisco on Highway One. When we arrived, I noticed first the smell—a combination of pine and warm grass and sea—and then the calming influence of the landscape. Rivulets of water were running through golden oceans of grass, surfacing at the edge of steep, flower-covered cliffs, and plunging to the beach below, surfacing once more where the sea rose to meet the sand. On the east side of Highway One, the meadows merged gradually into pine-covered hills that shift on the other side of the ridge into fragrant redwood forest through which the Little Gualala River runs. In a line I've heard in many versions from many people, I said to myself, "you've got to live here some day."

"Some day" took almost 15 years. Charles Moore, John Ruble, and Buzz Yudell were the architects for the new business school at Cal, the promise of which was one of the things that allowed me to leave my beloved Moore-designed museum at Dartmouth in 1989 to become director of the Berkeley Art Museum. Stephen Walrod, whom I married eight years later, shared my love for The Sea Ranch, and together we built a house here, finished in fall 1999. Moore Ruble Yudell had designed Stephen's Berkeley house; in fact, visiting that house was how Stephen and I got to know each other. Buzz and his wife Tina Beebe had a lot at The Sea Ranch, and our first thought was to build near them in a seaside meadow. In the process of making price comparisons, we came upon a hillside lot that sits above the far end of the little Sea Ranch airstrip. It has a 180-degree view of ocean and hills, a southern exposure, is protected at its northwest side by a gulchful of bishop pine, and at its back by a stately stand of firs. What really did it for me, though, was the airstrip:

my father had been a pilot. Stephen once referred to this place as my
"Oedipus complex."

When Buzz visited the site, he immediately dubbed an apse created by our stand of
Douglas fir the "sacred niche," and suggested that we design the house around it. He
pointed out that from this spot you can see white water. (It turns out that the waves
you see are the same waves that break on the rocks just to the north of Buzz and
Tina's house.) Before we saw each other again, Buzz did some sketches of how the
house might be laid out, and so did I. In plan, if not in skill level, they were almost
identical—a horizontal living space connected to a vertical work/guest space by a
breezeway. Together with our now legendary contractor Matt Sylvia, we created a
post and beam house with lots of porches, windows, and big glass doors. Despite all
the wood, it is a transparent house. Before it was begun, Stephen and I would picnic
on our hillside, fragrant with the pungent smell of Coyote Mint. We marveled at the
view and reveled in the warmth of the meadow and the cool darkness of the woods.
"It's too bad a house has to be built here," we told each other in mock distress.
The amazing thing is: it hasn't changed. There is a mantra here at The Sea Ranch:
"live lightly on the land." Sometimes, I feel like I'm levitating.

dwelling

making

manifesting

opening

choreographing

marking

III inhabiting *place*

climate	cycles
locale	movement
scales	discovery
landmark	light
fit	identity
water	community
earth	
sky	
regeneration	
center	
material	
detail	
color	

AS ARCHITECTS WE SHAPE PLACES BASED ON OUR UNDERSTANDING OF THE CULTURE, SITE, AND OUR SHARED ASPIRATIONS, BUT THEY ARE NOT FULLY REALIZED UNTIL THEY ARE INHABITED. Inhabitants are partners in a dynamic dialogue with buildings and sites. This interaction occurs in time and changes in subtle and dramatic ways with light, climate, season, and nature of community. We are also concerned with how elements of architecture can themselves inhabit the environment. How we make, craft, and populate our buildings with varying scales of details and objects is critical to their vitality.

A key to successful inhabiting is creating architecture that is strong enough to stimulate, challenge, and surprise, but quiet enough to allow, indeed encourage, the active unfolding of individual and communal life. We seek to make buildings which can be vessels for human experience, perception, and discovery: places which are full of wonder and strength but which are not so self-possessed or insistent as to limit or overwhelm a full range of emotional, sensate, and intellectual life.

The "fit" between building and inhabitants should be close enough to stimulate dialogue and loose enough to allow for individual creative experience.

Scales and Surrogates

We inhabit buildings with our bodies, and our buildings in turn inhabit their sites. Human and built habitation occurs at multiple scales. We interact with building as individuals, groups, and entire communities. Our buildings have relationships with their sites, contexts, and regions.

We also inhabit buildings through surrogates. These include representations of the human figure, miniatures of buildings, iconic elements, and an array of objects which have the power to stand for us.

30

31

32

33

34

The manipulation of scale in buildings, landscape, and objects heightens our awareness of our own spatial orientation. The perspective of the passage at the Villa di Papa Giulio in Rome is terminated by the unknowable scale of the figurative sculpture in the distance (fig. 30). This surrogate serves both to project us into distant space and to create tension and ambiguity in that spatial experience.

The miniature building at the baptistery of the Cathedral in Orvieto emphasizes the grandeur of the surrounding vaulted space (fig. 31). The giant figures astride Eliel Saarinen's train station in Helsinki hold illuminated globes and confer grandeur on the building and by extension on travel by train (fig. 32).

Some of the most affecting juxtapositions of scale occur in serendipitous fashion.

The visual surprise of the miniature house adjacent to fishing boats in Camoglie challenges both our sense of scale and the conventional understanding of building function and siting (fig. 33). The overlap of a stretch limousine with the diminutive California beach bungalow casts a startling light on our cultural understanding of affordability and value (fig. 34).

As we and surrogates occupy buildings and environments at multiple scales, we are challenged to see, experience, and understand in new and transformed persepectives.

Making and Crafting

The making of buildings in all their detail and materiality is central to the understanding and experience of place. Indeed, for our own design process, shaping material, detail, and color is a kind of habitation in itself: we begin to inhabit the rooms and places yet to be built, and to further invest those places with qualities that extend deeply into the experience of dwelling.

35

36

37

Our sense of making has evolved from a crossing of several inspiring sources. From Kahn, and in the early work of Moore Lyndon Turnbull Whitaker, there is the belief that the building has an inherent nature, that making is a process of becoming, and of being true to the deepest understanding of the building's purpose, rather than simply its function. Building systems and details grow outward from this core understanding of purpose, and are integrated by it. Designing churches, for example, has led us to see that all aspects of the making, from structural concepts to explicit ornament and art, can join in the celebration of liturgical purpose (fig. 35).

Another inspiration, and quite complimentary to Kahn, can be found in Bernard Maybeck's work: the spirited appropriation of things external to the program, site, or building type. If Kahn's approach becomes burdened by responsibility, Maybeck's inventiveness can be liberating. A classic example is his use of industrial sash windows and other manufactured, off-the-shelf products for the Christian Science Church in Berkeley. The sheer lightness of the sash plays beautifully against the weight of cast concrete and carved woodwork that characterize the interior.

The synthetic playfulness of Maybeck, Otto Wagner, Berlage, and other early modern masters of handcraft and industry continues to intrigue us. In designing for habitation, we seek a kind of organic, or perhaps ecological richness—the balance of dynamic forces. Structural systems can form symbiotic alliances, such as the artful assembly of steel trusses and masonry in the great hall of Berlage's Amsterdam Stock Exchange (fig. 36): the sweeping arch of structure passes from stone to steel as gracefully as the melody line passes from violin to clarinet in a Mozart concerto.

James Cutler's lovely Virginia Merrill Bloedel Education Center on Bainbridge Island (fig. 37), part private study, part personal memorial, presents a highly refined making in three parts—the stone base merging with the hillside, the light roof canopy

38

hovering over the rooms, and a timber frame lacing the two together. The architect's years of work refining his craft, carefully adding each invention to the whole, are self-evident: how the work is made speaks deeply of its purpose.

Making is more than detailing and execution—it is also about a way of conceiving. Kahn's famous offices for the scientists at the Salk Institute in La Jolla show how the making and crafting can be charged with purpose. These monastic units, from which the plan of the central courtyard is built up, have had some functional problems, but their meaning for habitation holds true: the moment when the researcher has an insight, looks up from her laptop, and walks to the balcony to gaze across the courtyard and out to the sea, letting her thoughts expand. All the qualities of the room, from its placement in space, to the elemental details of light and materials, are gathered to serve such an event. Making is habitation.

Elements and Cycles

The dynamic experience of place is animated and sustained through our interaction with the cycles of the natural world. These cycles in turn express a central duality: they manifest elemental physical principles which we experience as immutable, and they evolve through temporal cycles. Thus, our experience of nature through elements such as light, wind, water, and earth combines both a sense of the permanence of physical laws and the temporality of its expression.

Natural elements help us to understand and express the *genius loci*. As our natural world is increasingly threatened and as our lives are increasingly distanced from the natural elements, the importance of renewing our connection to the physical world is ever more critical. We cannot hope to be stewards of the earth if we are not intimately engaged in its cycles.

Architects have both explicitly and implicitly celebrated natural phenomena.

Nicola Salvi's Trevi Fountain (1732–1762) managed to celebrate the recently discovered cycles of water movement and evaporation, while creating one of the great enduring places that nurture public life. The fountains of Moorish gardens leveraged the scarcity of water into a sophisticated design schema for irrigation; the very preciousness of water becoming the basis of a tectonic and aesthetic program. In these examples, our connection to the element and cycles of water is a source of symbolic and experiential engagement. Contrast this with an infrastructure that does its best to bury and hide its workings, so that our connection to the movement of water is limited to turning the tap.

Similarly, we tend to ignore the patterns of air movement unless we find ourselves in extreme environments. Mechanically treated air systems have lulled us into accepting sealed and tempered boxes as the default design for most new buildings. The energy sector is the single largest source of carbon dioxide emissions in the world, accounting for about 40 percent of all global warming emissions. As a conse-

39

quence, nearly half of greenhouse gas emissions in industrial countries are attributable to the energy consumption of buildings.

Most vernacular traditions developed sophisticated ways of building in harmony with the environment. The medieval houses of Cairo combine the insulation of massive walls, solar shading, and the cooling of convection and evaporation to temper a harsh climate. All this is done with the parallel development of a rich spatial language (fig. 38).

At the Sea Ranch, Esherick's hedgerow houses are clustered, nestled into the earth and shaped to deflect the powerful coastal wind and storms (fig. 39). The Swim and Tennis Club II of MLTW achieves an elegant beauty by shaping the earth as a three-sided wind dam and the building as a buttressed wall on the fourth side of the recreational areas. Even as the building as "wall" inhabits the land, the visitors inhabit the wall itself in spaces that are safe from the wind, but that reach up to the sky and the light.

Light is perhaps the element to which architects have paid the greatest homage. From the nearly ecstatic spatial complexity of the baroque, to the ordered and sublime spaces of Louis Kahn, to the spare sensuous beauty of Luis Barragan, they have shaped their buildings to receive light and interact with its diurnal and seasonal cycles.

The longer cycles of life are less often considered. Ironically, real estate development does address this through financing: buildings are often amortized over 20 years, discouraging the investment in more sustainable and permanent materials and construction. Alternately, some institutions decide to build higher quality buildings as 50- or 100-year buildings. The new Cathedral of Los Angeles by Rafael Moneo has been designed as a 500-year building, a nearly unique commitment in contemporary construction.

40

One of the few cultures that embraces both the transience and the complexities of time and aging is Japan. The Shrine at Ise is completely rebuilt every 20 years—a generation—with the ceremonial burning of the last shrine even as the new building rises to represent both permanence and change. At Ryoanji Temple in Kyoto a 500-year-old wall is admired for its beauty and is an object of meditation as powerful as any altar, as mysterious as a Rothko painting.

In many ways we are driven by time and the imperatives of an institutionalized process of building. As architects, we continue to look for ways to remember and connect to the natural cycles and elements. In this way we can inhabit the world by engaging its physicality and temporality.

Choreographing and Sensing

One of the great joys of architecture is its ability to engage the mind as well as all of the senses. As architects, we are naturally affected by our education and our immersion in the cultural environment. Our education is largely visual and verbal and our media are increasingly visual and electronic. There is a natural bias, therefore, toward these modes of understanding and expression. There is a certain inertial tendency to create architecture of the head over architecture of the body. Robert Venturi has spoken of much recent architecture as "frozen theory," a play on the historical reference to architecture as "frozen music."

To engage less than all the senses is to limit understanding and experience. The movement of our bodies through space and time, and the complementary kinesthetic and tactile senses, are central to the active inhabiting of places. We understand space and proportion in relation to our bodies. We sense the materiality of environments through our bodies.

Humanistic traditions in architecture have understood this over millennia.

In Greek architecture, the body became the template from which proper proportions were derived. The Renaissance reasserted a body-centered system of composition. Even the iconoclastic modernist, Le Corbusier, embraced this tradition with his "Modulor" proportioning system. Vernacular architecture has typically been embedded with an understanding of the tactile experience of building and inhabiting.

While a concern for proportion is still alive in architecture, there is less discussion about how bodies fit, move through, and sense buildings. This active and sensate experience of place occurs at multiple scales and in multiple modes.

The choreography of human movement takes place in buildings, on sites, in landscapes, and cities, and increasingly across vast distances through car, train, and air travel. We are perhaps more aware than ever of distance, speed, and global geography. Yet, ironically, we probably move our bodies less in a typical day than before high-speed transportation. If we compare a day spent in Urbino, moving through its topographic richness, and a day spent in a suburban office complex in 9-foot-high boxes of space, we can only wonder about what experiences we are erasing from our lives.

Fortunately, some of the more expressive contemporary architects are re-energizing the choreographic opportunities of architecture. Frank Gehry's Bilbao Museum celebrates dynamic movement both on the urban scale and at the scale of bodies moving through space (fig. 40). The exuberant manipulation of light only serves to enhance the spatial and choreographic experience. Ricardo Legoretta has shown us how an understanding of traditional proportion and materiality can be reinterpreted to create humane and sensuous contemporary places (fig. 41).

Our movement through space is not only the basis of individual experience and understanding, it can support and amplify our social interactions. A rich network of spatial movement in a city or a building contributes demonstrably to the level of social and creative interaction. Even research into organizational performance has demonstrated the importance of movement and serendipitous interaction to both creativity and productivity.

As architects, we can shape places that encourage a range of ways of fitting into and moving through space (fig. 42). This in turn heightens our understanding of ourselves in relation to others, to environments, and to the cycles of nature.

Marking

Landmarks are essential to our inhabiting at the largest scale: the city and landscape. Whether natural or constructed, landmarks establish a spatial order that is different from other kinds of order, and that engages and activates our memory. The recognition and remembering of landmarks provide the foundation of our complex cognitive maps of places, and reinforce the identification with place that is part of our individual and collective identities. To inhabit a region is to know its landmarks (fig. 43).

41

42

43 44 45

While most landmarks are large, and usually tall, marking reinforces habitation at a variety of scales and has but one requirement: that the marker is memorable when viewed relative to its surroundings. Marking, therefore, has to do with placement, scale, proportion, contrast, and gesture. Landmarks achieve a kind of unity, even when composed of multiple parts like New York's Rockefeller Center. Landmark places are created by subtraction, such as Piazza San Marco in Venice, but usually are then reinforced by further marking: by the campanile, the Duomo, fountains, sculpture, and landscape.

We think of marking in relation to habitation, in part because it is a cultural phenomenon. The classic Mediterranean stance—the white or brightly colored building, suddenly upright in the landscape—uses opposition to establish and celebrate a human presence. The Chinese landmark—such as the Temple of Heaven in Beijing (fig. 44), may be just as tall or colorful, but it mediates its presence through a system of walls, walks, and platforms spreading into the surrounding landscape, exhaustively integrating the marker and the context.

Further still from the western model, the great temple of Borobudur, on the island of Java (fig. 45), stands as a kind of manmade land form. Set among hills, the monument's tiered stacking of nearly identical terraces lined with hundreds of virtually identical stupas—each with an identical Buddha inside—marks the human presence through a kind of appropriation and transformation of the landscape itself.

Within our own culture, the need for landmarks manifests itself in both the positive forms of buildings, and the spatial identification of important places. UCLA's central campus features a grand cross-axis of original buildings that establishes a definitive character for the campus as a whole. The landmark quality of the space is achieved by the distance between buildings and their capacity to speak across that distance by means of towers, porches, loggias, the material patterns of red brick and sandstone, and roof profiles.

46

Elsewhere in the Los Angeles region, the opportunities and the need for markers exists at a grand scale. Antoine Predock's great wedge-tower at Cal Poly Pomona establishes the identity of the campus at the super-monumental scale and high speed of the San Bernadino Freeway, and the Getty Museum, while not as singular, makes a similar statement of regional culture on the 405 freeway.

Even the typical "citadel" of downtown commerce, a cluster of office towers, helps to demarcate a region and provides a focus of orientation in the messy sprawl of most American cities. Remarkable from an architectural viewpoint is the fact that only one or two distinguished buildings—in Los Angeles the Library Place Tower by Harry Cobb and the Gas Company Tower of Richard Keating/SOM—can be powerful enough to bring the entire, relatively uninspired collection together into some kind of memorable whole: a lucky example of the value of the marker in our visually oriented environment (fig. 46).

Tango, Bo01 Housing Exhibition
Malmö, Sweden

Bo01, City of Tomorrow, is an ambitious demonstration of sustainable community planning and housing design, which had its public opening in the Spring of 2001. From the re-use of its industrial waterfront site—a classic "brown field"—to its ultimate goal of complete self-sufficiency—the approximately 1400 units of housing will not depend on Malmö's power or utility grid—Bo01 sets out to be a model of 21st-century development. And unlike many of Sweden's annual housing exhibitions, Bo01 is also a permanent settlement, built by public/private investment.

While it is contemporary in execution and spirit, the master plan by Swedish architect Klas Tham is a delicately scaled, pedestrian-only village, with a strong perimeter definition—a kind of modern walled town. With the sea on two sides, and a new canal lining the other two, Bo01 is also an island, which heightens the sense of the site as reclaimed artificial land. We were invited by our Potatisåkern clients to join Bertil Öhrström of FFNS Malmö to design a small, 27-unit block along the canal.

Mediating the Elements
The Bo01 site feels exposed—the coast at the Öresund is often cold, wet, and windy—and the town's walled perimeter has important psychological if not physi-

cal advantages for habitation. One side of Tango forms part of this four-story town wall.

Wall and Pavilion
The town plan's quality of protected enclosure—a tough outside with a soft interior—was compelling enough that we were moved to shape Tango along similar lines: a wall building tautly wraps three sides of a south-facing court. The external construction is rusticated and durable—ribbed pre-cast concrete panels alternate with narrow floor-to-ceiling windows to make a lively but unified façade. From the protection of the walls, glassy bays project out for views and light. Within the courtyard, a set of glass pavilions, like small towers, are gathered around a garden.

Freedom and Choice
Given Tango's direct, self-evident concept—wall wraps court—we wanted to set things in motion. The glass towers of different heights declare their independence from the wall by turning slightly as they step around the court—a dance-like movement that inspired our Swedish colleagues to give the project its name. Inside, every apartment has a piece of the wall and part of a glass tower—the tower rooms for living, and the wall spaces divided into bedrooms and baths.
>>>>

Tango's plan and color idea are simultaneous.

The canal façade is set in motion by each unit's unique window placement.   >>>>

The "intelligent wall"—in red—is common to all units.

Each plan is unique, a special combination and shaping of repeated components, which offers the inhabitants highly individual choices.

I.T. for Modern Living

One interesting feature common to all the plans is another wall—an Intelligent Wall. Framed of demountable cabinetry, it runs through the middle of the plan and provides each unit with the cabling and services of a custom-designed information system. While offering programs to enhance future lifestyles—integrated vacation planning and away-from-home care, for example—Tango's custom network also monitors the details of power and energy use throughout the day—a treasury of information to help residents

and the management streamline their energy profile—an eminently sustainable idea.

Color Garden

At the center of the Tango community is a courtyard garden, framed and energized by a Mondrianesque color scheme. The garden itself restates Bo01's ethos as island amid the marshlands: a small elliptical terrace set into a wet garden of mosses and tall grasses, linked to the building by a set of wooden bridges. Private balconies overlook the court, just a few meters from each other: the assumption is, and so far it seems to be working, that anyone unusual enough to live in Tango is going to have some very interesting neighbors!

Glassy bays step and turn about the courtyard.

Glass towers of different heights declare their independence by turning slightly as they step around the court.

Photovoltaic panels and sod cover large areas of the roof surface.

The small elliptical terrace is linked to the buildings by wooden bridges, spanning a "wetland" of grasses. >>>>

Each unit has a portion of a glass tower with a unique orientation and view.

Yudell/Beebe House
The Sea Ranch, California

This house was developed in close response to the rhythms and materials of the rugged coast of Northern California. Close to a coastal bluff, the site falls under strict architectural guidelines. We sought to embrace the fundamental environmental intentions of the guidelines while creating a contemporary place of strong individual character and quiet complexity.

Living in the Land
Each part of the house responds to its specific site conditions. The east elevation presents a rugged entry, a contemporary interpretation of the "western front." The south opens to the ocean with full or partial shading. The west screens the interior from houses across the meadow while framing water and rocks through habitable bays. The north is shaped as an intimate court with mountain views. A garden of native grasses and rocks suggests the connection of mountain to ocean. The movement and transparency through the heart of the house complete this spatial link.

Moving through Light and Space
Movement through and around the house is choreographed to enhance the spatial and sensate experience. Spaces are shaped simply in plan, yet shift dramatically in height and present a lay-

ered sequence of framed views and paths. The building form and exterior spaces define each other in dynamic dialogue.

Windows are composed to frame near and distant landscapes and to celebrate the movement and wash of light. The northeast-facing courtyard catches the morning sun and screens prevailing winds. The towers of the studios collect light and enhance convection. They are markers in the landscapes while meeting the 16-foot height limit. The house is configured as a one-room-deep array so that all spaces have multiple exposures, optimizing daylight and ventilation.

In harmony with its environment, the house celebrates craft and materials and shapes a retreat for quiet contemplation or spirited social interaction.

The house mediates the transition from forested hills to ocean bluffs.   >>>>

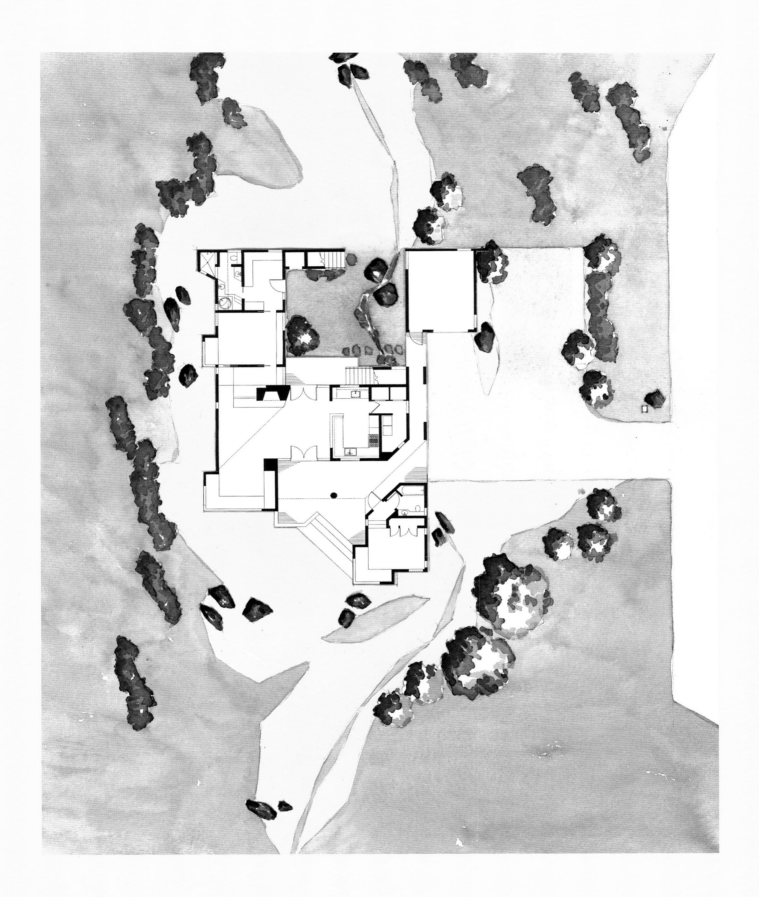

The northeast-facing courtyard catches the
morning sun and protects from prevailing
winds.

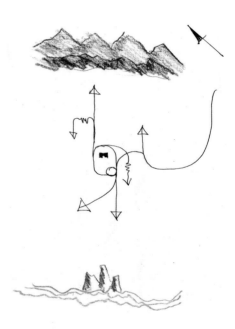

Movement through and around the house is choreographed

to enhance the spatial and sensate experience.

Windows are composed to frame near and
distant landscapes and to celebrate the
movement and wash of light.

The east elevation (below) presents a rugged entry, a contemporary interpretation of the "western front."

coloring: expanding and defining

Tina Beebe

WHEN CONCEIVED AS PART OF THE DEVELOPING DESIGN CONCEPT, THE CHOICES OF COLOR AND MATERIALS HAVE UNIQUE POTENTIAL TO EXPAND AND DEFINE PHYSICAL AS WELL AS INTELLECTUAL ASPECTS OF ARCHITECTURE. Two recent projects which illustrate this process in very different ways are the Tango apartments in Malmö, Sweden and our house at The Sea Ranch, California.

As part of a large urban redevelopment site along the waterfront of Malmö, Sweden, Tango is a single block of 27 apartment units. From the earliest conceptual diagram, it was clear that color could have a powerful role in developing the spatial possibilities of the overall plan and in the individual units. As a result, color has been so thoroughly integrated into the design that it is inseparable from the building's expression.

Cool Outside, Hot Inside

A quiet palette of neutral colors, intended to be courteous neighbors, defines the perimeter walls of the complex. Inside, the more private interior courtyard towers dance in a riot of strong clear colors. Glassy living room towers separate from the main mass of the building and rotate at various angles around an elliptical garden courtyard. Each of the eight towers is exuberantly defined by a unique and vibrant hue. These include a warm and a cool each of red, blue, and yellow, with the added complements of a mineral green and a deep blue violet. Though each color is different in hue, they are all similar in intensity, making a clear family of colors.

Syncopated Rhythm

The sense of dynamic movement created by the rotation in plan of the square towers is increased by the intensity of the colors. Each of the towers seems to gain a sense of being an individual unit while being part of a lively and eclectic neighborhood.

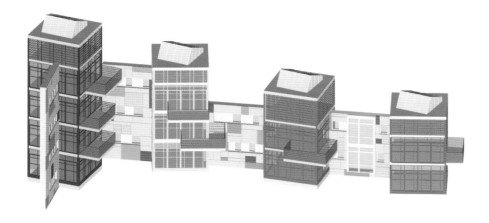

The vibrant colors on the towers create a visual separation from the lightly colored walls behind them. Elevations of the main building wall are scored in a Mondrian-like pattern of irregular rectangles. A few of these rectangles are defined by one of the eight tower colors, creating a rhythm of movement among the rectangles and between the glassy towers and solid walls.

A series of uniquely shaped semi-private small garden spaces are composed of plant materials carefully chosen to complement the tower colors. They are reminiscent of the marshy wetland that once covered this area and establish an ecosystem that purifies rainwater draining from the site.

Like the traditional fishing villages of Sweden where houses were brightly painted to be visible from out at sea, the intense colors read from a distance and welcome the residents to their homes. Tango occupants identify with the color of their towers and describe their location by color rather than by a number. In the grey Swedish climate the cheerful reds, ochres, and blues remind the Swedes that summer is not far off and will come again.

Fitting the Land

At The Sea Ranch on the foggy northern coast of California, it too often seems that summer is far off. Unlike in Sweden, vibrant exterior color has no role to play here. The guiding architectural aesthetic is that of the old weathered barns found on the original ranch, and like the old barns, new houses are meant to feel a part of the land both in shape and color.

Redwood was traditionally the preferred material for siding and roofs, but since this preference is no longer a sustainable option, a number of more renewable materials are being used. Much of the serenity of the development accrues from this very lim-

ited palette of weathered wood siding and neutral organic paint color on window mullions and occasionally doors. Consequently, the opportunity to apply color apart from these happens only on the interiors of houses, or perhaps in enclosed court-yards where they cannot be seen from the exterior.

In our house at The Sea Ranch the exterior palette is made up of redwood siding left to weather naturally to the silvery gray of the old barns, with windows, doors, and roof of metal painted a deep soft gray. The gray concrete base was washed with a brownish stain to meld it with the redwood. These mellow indigenous colors on the exterior give way on the inside to a much brighter and more intense palette, yet still rooted in colors of the surrounding natural environment.

Expressing Materials

Fir ceilings and doors, beech cabinets, and a hemlock floor are left natural and con-tinue the exterior woodiness. Plaster walls are tinted with powdered pigments incompletely mixed in to yield the streaks and splotches of a natural material. Pig-ment suspended in plaster rather than evenly applied to the surface gives a sense of depth and something of the solidity of stone. We added a sunny ochre pigment to the typical wall color to connect with views of dried meadow grasses of summer. The fireplace plaster incorporates coffee to soften the white plaster to a warm (and speckled) earthy taupe, similar to the limestone hearth. Accent walls in the living area are tinted the yellow greens of lichen-covered rock and the blue greens of tufts of native grass. Bathroom walls mirror the ever-changing watery hues of the blue-green Pacific beyond. For our studio accent walls, Buzz chose a very saturated Italian ochre for his, and I chose its complement—an Yves Klein cobalt blue.

Adding Intensity

Fabrics and furniture are the only truly bright color accents, and these are based on the native wildflowers. The deep purple-blue of the hardy Pacific coast iris, singing Indian yellow of the California poppy, and a cadmium orange from the fiery Indian paintbrush decorate pillows and chairs. A few pale yellowy greens from the mosses and lichens also appear in fabrics and tiles.

In the courtyard garden, an intensified "high key" version of the native meadows beyond has been chosen. Brilliant lime green Irish moss covers the banks of a virtual stream composed of gray-green rocks of all sizes carried in, a few at a time, from local beaches. In winter, excess rainfall fills the stream bed, but in summer, cobalt blue beach glass vibrates with the orange poppies along the edge. Where the virtual stream appears on the meadow side, it is defined as a brilliant river of blue native iris in the spring.

The rationale behind choices for color and materials may seem mysterious, intangible or even arbitrary. But when these choices are informed by the site, the building, the users, and the environment, they can broaden and deepen the meaning and experience of buildings in a profound way. Color possesses the unique ability to expand design intent and to define formative influences.

Regatta Wharf Housing at Jackson's Landing
Sydney, Australia

Sydney, far and away one of the world's most delightful residential cities, owes its grandeur and charm to the harbor: a rich shoreline geography of alternating headlands and coves. Around each cove a beautifully scaled neighborhood tumbles down a lushly landscaped hillside to a small beach, where an elegant local restaurant has taken over an old pavilion next to the park. Around Circular Quay, at one of the larger coves, Sydney gathers its renowned collection of landmarks: the Opera House, Sydney Harbour Bridge, and the rugged, historic neighborhood known as The Rocks.

Further in along the waterfront, past the splashy tourist attractions of Darling Harbor, is the older industrial district of Pyrmont, where an enormous sugar mill site has been re-planned as a high-end residential development—"Jackson's Landing."

Belvedere
As a foreground to the project, occupying the choicest cut of its real estate, Regatta Wharf has been shaped according to the prime directive of Sydney housing development: capture the view. We sought to heighten the experience of living at the water's edge in Sydney's mild climate by providing each unit in the 250-unit complex with not just a balcony, but a generous veranda—a real outdoor room. The verandas are a high-rise interpretation of the classic Australian porch, complete with power and gas for the barbeque. The verandas are stacked at corners or wrap around living rooms, giving an inside-outside laciness to the large mass of the towers.

Rugged Refinement
The towers cluster around two courts, one centered on a circular mound and fountain, and the other offering a narrow stepped garden from the street down to the waterfront promenade. Between the two tower groups a small park looks out to the harbor and back to the great stone bluff, through which a dramatic stairway has been chiseled.

The massive, cut rock walls behind Regatta Wharf, and the industrial heritage of the site's context inspired spare, solid walls with punched windows on façades facing the bluff, in complete contrast to the louver-and-glass openness of the waterfront elevations. These opposing aspects mirror our own outsider's view of two keynotes of Australian culture—the tautly pragmatic realism and the studied appreciation of the finer things in life.

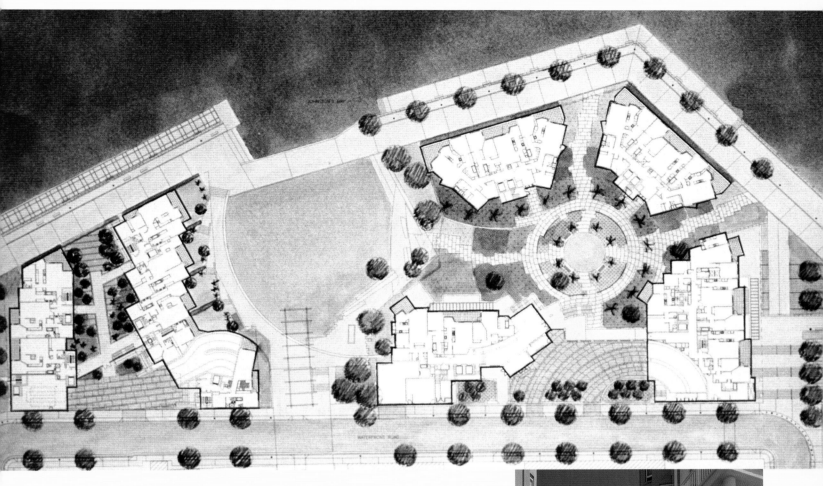

Bridges float through the garden, linking the towers to street and waterfront.

Open verandas draw the harbor into each dwelling.

The Student Life Center, University of Cincinnati
Cincinnati, Ohio

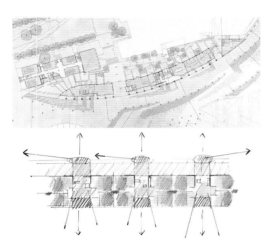

The Student Life Center and the renovated Swift Hall are part of a new spine of campus activity organized along major pedestrian and topographic paths. The project is part of a multi-building "Main Street" planned collaboratively within a campus master plan by Hargreaves Associates. It is anchored at one end by Gwathmey-Siegel's Tangeman Center and at the other by a new student recreation center designed by Morphosis. The Student Life Center links the two along a thin curving site, traversing nearly 600 feet in length and 55 feet of vertical drop.

The dense mix of academic, social, and retail uses provides the community with a district of activity and urbanity not found within most campuses.

Arc of Interaction
The Center evolved as a vessel for movement and interaction. It traverses the site as a long slender form, which encourages parallel movement along a south-facing arcade. Student amenities and organizations have identities and entries along the arcade. The most active day/night uses, such as cafés and computer labs, are located at street level. Key paths of campus movement are reinforced by perpendicular cuts, literally short cuts through the building. A series of "found spaces" to the north are shaped as social places between the new building and existing buildings. To the west a covered atrium is formed between the Center and the older Swift Hall.

Body Language
This collection of spaces adjacent to buildings provides a diversity of domains in which to gather, perch, and move. They celebrate the pleasures of topographic movement and present a wide range of scales, thus heightening one's kinesthetic awareness.

The Center itself is a single-loaded building with social corridors along the south side. These recapitulate the movement of the arcade below and are animated by bays for informal gathering. Social stairs are daylit and become focal points for orientation and movement. The building form and fenestration are animated by the activities within. Bays, galleries, and arcades speak of the dynamic academic and social energy of the place.

Tectonics of Earth and Sky
The Center will be built of simple, direct construction. It meets and merges with the earth though a combination of cast-in-place concrete and brick at the arcade. A light zinc and glass skin emphasizes horizontal movement and reflects the sky. Metal sunscreens protect the major south-facing gathering spaces. A program of boldly colored signage will identify and animate the social role of the building.

The Center connects to the campus at multiple scales though axial movements, framed views, and positively configured open spaces.

A richness of habitation arises, in part, from the diversity of scale of places, between, adjacent to, and inside the buildings. These present an array of spaces, articulated enough to invite habitation, yet flexible and subtle enough for the participants to improvise and vary their scale and type of activity. From the window bay for one or two, to a quiet mews terrace, to the large enclosure of the atrium or sweep of the arcade, the inhabitant is engaged in a dynamic interaction with the building and its greater campus setting.

A covered atrium is formed between the Center
and the older Swift Hall.

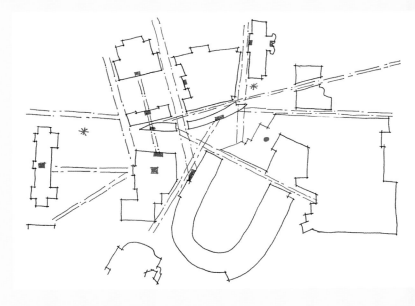

Key paths of campus movement are reinforced
by perpendicular cuts through the building.

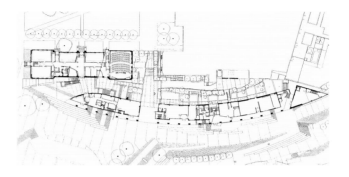

Anchored at one end by Gwathmey Siegel's
Tangeman Center and at the other by a new
Morphosis building, the Student Life Center
links the two along a thin curving site.

Hugh & Hazel Darling Law Library Addition
Univerisity of California, Los Angeles

The UCLA Law School had grown somewhat casually since its founding in 1949. Successive additions had barely met technical needs, with little thought about the synergy between each new element and the whole. With almost no available land, and under Campus Architect Duke Oakley's direction, it was felt that a residual space at the southwest corner of the school could be leveraged to make a strong identity for the Law School and emphasize the entry to the historic axis of campus development.

Campus Landmark
The design evolved as a combination of a strong corner tower on the southeast and a layer of new library program enfronting the whole eastern edge of the site. The building now presents a strong school and campus identity as visitors enter from Circle Drive to the north. To the south and west, it steps down to create habitable terraces for new faculty offices and a new south-facing entry courtyard with quiet seating and an accessible entry for both the new and old building. Internally, the addition emphasizes the clarity of organization for the expanded library collection.

The library is composed of places of tranquility and movement, contained "rooms" of space, free-flowing spaces, and places that function at multiple scales for individuals, group study, and events. There is a clear gradient of public to private uses: the formal renovated main reading room and other public areas are located on the main level adjacent to the collection, while more secluded study areas at upper levels provide space primarily for the Law School community.

Climbing to Views and Light
While quiet study spaces are lit with washes of natural light, a sculptural social stair is intensely colored and brightly lit by recessed skylights. At the top, the tower reading room has become an iconic space used for study, celebration, and fundraising. It provides a panoramic prospect from downtown to the mountains and ocean. After dusk it becomes the lantern, which identifies the Law School across the campus.

The materials and craft of the building connect to and reinterpret the established campus palette. Brick, pre-cast concrete and terracotta relate to the immediate district but are rendered with more graphic and rhythmic variation than the existing law school. Inside, a quiet palette of natural woods is crafted for serenity and durability. Warm, deep colors and washes of light provide contrast and animation.

Intimate gardens are carved into the building's east side. Here native landscape connects interior reading spaces to distant views.

The social stair is intensely colored and animated by recessed skylights.   >>>>

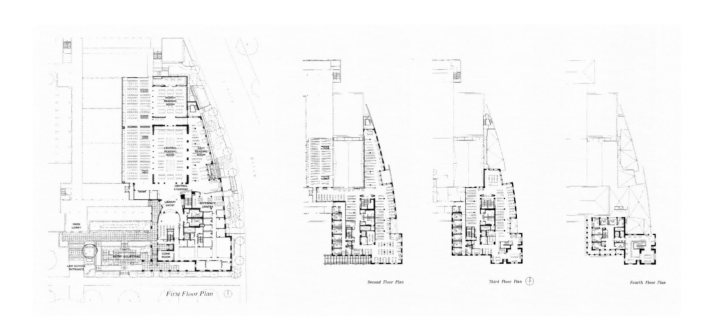

First Floor Plan

Second Floor Plan

Third Floor Plan

Fourth Floor Plan

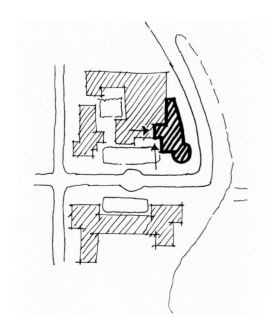

The library curves and steps down along the entry drive.

After dusk, the tower becomes the lantern that identifies the law school.

The formal renovated main reading room.

The library is composed of places of tranquility and movement, contained "rooms" of space, free flowing spaces, and places that function at multiple scales for individuals, group study, and events.

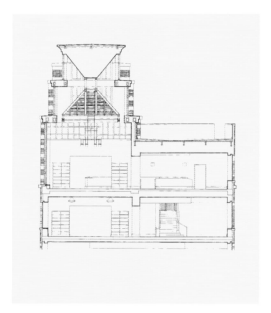

The tower reading room has become an iconic
space for study and celebration.

Horace Mann Elementary School
San Jose, California

Diagonally across the street from the site of San Jose's gigantic new City Hall—a not yet realized design by Richard Meier—is the neighborhood's new elementary school. In recognition of the context, the Community Redevelopment Agency called for a more substantial building than the School District's usual rock-bottom budget would provide, and were willing to put up the funds for it. The program for classes K-6 was also augmented to have a multi-purpose hall, and other public-serving facilities, making the school and its playgrounds more of an all-around community center.

Simultaneous Translation
We wanted to have public design input, and the mixed Latino/Southeast Asian community showed up enthusiastically: our first tri-lingual design workshop! It was an unforgettable thrill to see that, after some initial head-scratching,

teams of families and neighbors passionately argued in their various languages, and became deeply engrossed in laying out the school site using foam blocks and colored paper. They soon focused on practical issues like preserving open space for play areas, and enclosing outdoor spaces for security and control. Indeed, open space versus building was a challenging dilemma on the 3-acre site.

Law of the Indies
Central San Jose had been laid out according to the Law of the Indies, the historic Spanish Colonial planning code that called for decorum and careful proportion in the arrangements of new towns. We wanted the school to have an analogous sense of order in the way that buildings framed public space in the half-city-block campus. After many alternatives we came to a three-story building scheme which, like some of the workshop designs, hugs the northern edge of the site, partly screening the mass of a taller parking structure across the street. The school library and the multipurpose hall hold the corners along East Santa Clara Street, framing a front garden around an enormous redwood tree. Rooftop play areas and outdoor circulation galleries are linked to the ground by sculptural, open stairways, making the building circulation system

almost entirely visible from the central courtyard.

Civility Without Pretense
The civic character of the school, a quality not emphasized in the school district's recent campuses, was realized by playing up the scale of the multi-purpose hall, library, and three-story classroom wing, and by using modest but durable materials—ground-face colored concrete block for exterior walls, and sloped roofs and upper wall panels of metal. Most importantly, the school's varied open spaces are finely delineated with canopy-covered walks, allées of trees, solid masonry walls, and the building walls, giving character and significance to all parts of this urban campus.

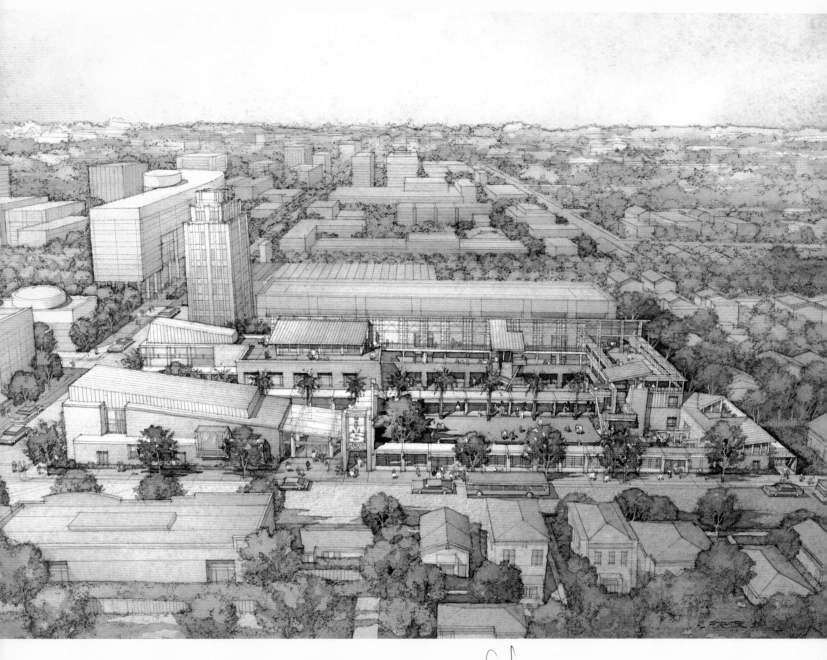

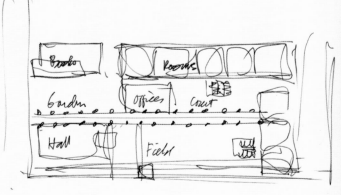

The dense urban campus mixes educational
and community uses.

Exterior circulation reveals patterns of movement.

Manzanita Village
University of California, Santa Barbara

The architecture of this residential village is shaped to enhance and express community at multiple scales. In response to a site where the campus meets the ocean, we inflected the typologies of the courtyard and the urban square to establish strong social places and connect to the power of the landscape.

Major axes of movement through the project link to the adjacent housing and campus patterns beyond. Active pedestrian paths intersect at a central plaza where housing, dining, and academic uses all have a strong presence and identity. The north-south paseo visually links to the mountains and the ocean. The east-west paseo strategically links a public entry off Ocean Road through the village and to the lagoon.

Anchoring and Inflecting

The village connects to its environment in multiple ways. The exterior paths and courtyards are shaped both to contain community and to orient toward the landscape. Building massing is highest at the central plaza and steps down toward the bluff and lagoon. In plan, the buildings are organized on the campus grid. They are anchored at the central plaza, but inflect as they move out into the landscape to create a more varied set of experiences and views. This duality of being anchored yet moving into the

landscape reminds us of natural phenomena, such as kelp or seaweed, whose movement in the water is more varied toward the periphery.

Balancing the Individual and the Community

The buildings are conceived as a three-dimensional "social-plaid," encouraging more dynamic social interaction. Social magnets and amenities, such as lounges, studies, kitchens, and laundries, are collected into hubs of activity.

Students can realize their identity at a range of scales. They occupy single or double rooms. Between 40 and 60 students occupy a typical "house" with full amenities. Six houses compose each of three quads, accommodating about 270 students each. All 800 students share dining, recreational, and academic facilities with the existing San Rafael housing to the north.

We were interested in shaping buildings as simple, clear volumes whose details and color occur in socially and environmentally meaningful ways. Entryways, social hubs, bays, and porches are richly articulated. Individual room windows are celebrated with colored awnings according to solar orientation.

〉〉〉〉

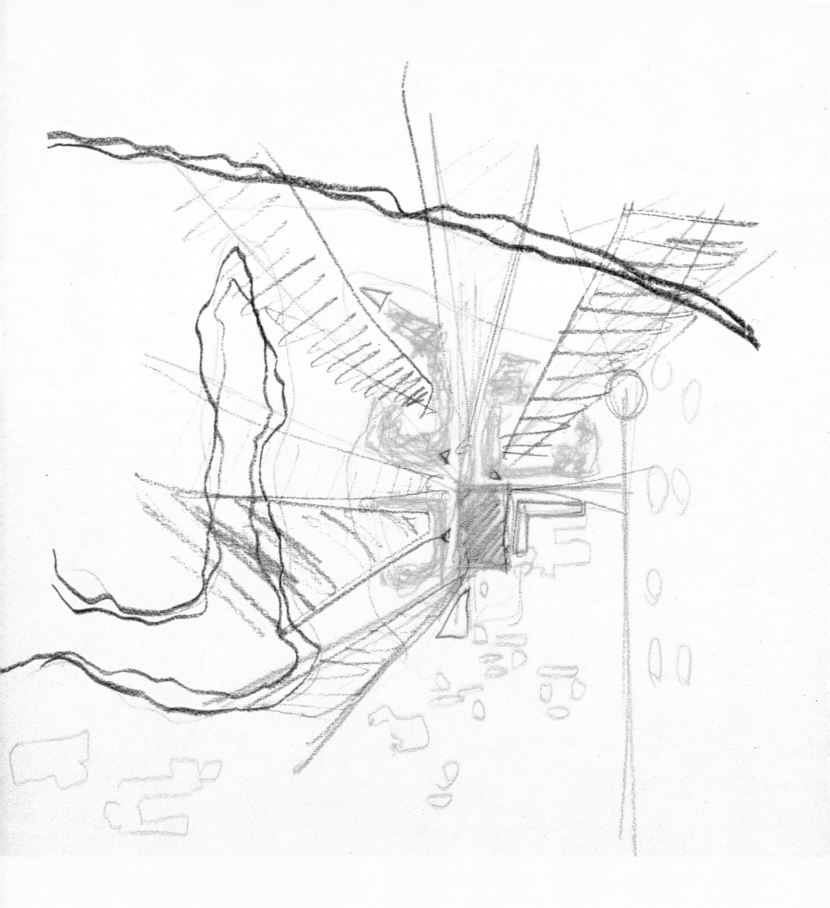

Major views and axes of movement help to
shape community.

Tina Beebe's color palette is developed in a close response to the landscape. The western quad is based on the palette of the nearby Eucalyptus hedgerow. The southeast quad recalls the colors of sand driftwood and the beach beyond. The northern quad is inspired by the colors of the lagoon to which it is oriented. The communal dining and academic buildings are more intensely colored, symbolic of the vibrancy of the activity within, yet related to the palettes of the housing. The large white building planes unify the whole village. The color restates the social goals of lively diversity within a harmonious whole.

Katie Spitz's landscape plan incorporates a spectrum of materials: from urban at the central plaza to restored native grasses at the periphery. Sustainability is enhanced through the use of drought-tolerant planting, bio-swales, permeable paving, and recycled water.

Connecting to the campus, respecting the extraordinary natural site, and supporting a range of social experience has informed our effort to establish a supportive framework for the expression of the individual and the growth of community.

Clear simple volumes are animated by sun
shades, stairways, and "social bays."

Movement is expressed and celebrated.

Great effort was made to balance individuality and community.

The buildings are conceived as a three-dimensional "social-plaid"

encouraging more dynamic social interaction.

Indoor and outdoor dining animates the
central plaza.   >>>>

Dining and gathering spaces are varied and informal.

Building massing steps down from the central plaza toward the bluff and lagoon. >>>>

Six houses compose each of three quads.

People moved here, made a new start and really wanted to achieve something

Miller Stevens

Karow-Nord, Ten Years Later*

Mr. Volker Kaiser and his family moved to Karow-Nord in 1994. When he first viewed the four-room apartment, the entire development was more of a construction site. Nonetheless, he was excited about the emerging neighborhood, the new schools for his two daughters and the brand new apartment.

When Mr. Kaiser speaks of the "pioneer spirit" that characterized the early years in Karow-Nord, his eyes take on a glaze. He was one of the founding members of the local sports club that brought and continues to bring together many residents of the new development but from the old village as well. Even if he doesn't manage to play as much soccer as before, the various activities in the club keep him and his family busy (and healthy).

Despite some of the problems he associates with Karow-Nord—traffic to and from town, certain shortcomings in the retail offerings and a general complacency following the euphoria of the first years—Mr. Kaiser will probably remain a Karower. When his oldest daughter recently looked for an apartment of her own, her move took her only a few blocks away to an above-shop unit along the Querspange.

Mrs. Annita Röstel moved to Karow in 1999 and lives in an MRY building adjacent to the commercial Querspange. Former neighbors from her previous apartment in the inner city were skeptical about her move to the new development but lost all doubts after their first visit. Even her son, who was beforehand reluctant about his parents' move, is convinced they made a great decision. Mrs. Röstel has become a bonafide New Karower and vows she'll never move again: "Leave? Only in a coffin."

From her third-floor apartment Mrs. Röstel looks down on the square where an open-air market is held twice a week. She refers to it as the piazza—with all its positive connotations—rather than calling it by its German name, Platz. One of the greatest advantages of the new development is the "fresh air and sunlight"—it's a bit like being in the country and yet Alexanderplatz is only 35 minutes away with

*Karow-Nord, a 5000-unit mixed-use development in Berlin Weissensee, was master planned by Moore Ruble Yudell in 1992. The architectural design was completed by Moore Ruble Yudell and some 20 other firms during the next seven years.

public transportation. In Karow it truly is easy to walk among the wheat fields or to the nearby nature preserve with its ponds and still enjoy your gelato on the piazza afterwards.

Mrs. Sabine Junge has been the director of one of the two elementary schools in Karow-Nord since it opened in 1996. In the first months of operation, the school had few pupils since most the housing was in the final phase of construction. She, too, remembers the dust and trucks.

While Mrs. Junge may have a different type of relationship to the new neighborhood than the residents, she is keenly aware of the social developments. She and her young colleagues have created a family-like atmosphere in the school which attracts pupils from beyond Karow. Through the combined efforts with active parents they have succeeded in establishing, in addition to the local sports club, an after-school group and a lunch program.

The school has become perhaps the social center for all the residents of Karow-Nord. Through the various non-school activities such as concerts and movies, the school has moved well beyond its role as a place just for learning. Mrs. Junge explains the generally high motivation in Karow as follows: "People moved here, made a new start and really wanted to achieve something."

For Mrs. Junge, Karow-Nord is unique among the housing developments of the recent past. The initially anticipated tension between the old village of Karow and Karow-Nord has not materialized, today the two enjoy more of a peaceful coexistence. Its appropriate scale, the well-built houses, the "charming" apartments and, last but not least, the elementary school will help Karow-Nord remain unique.

biographies

John Ruble, FAIA

John Ruble began his career as architect and planner in the Peace Corps, Tunisia, where a profound experience of culture, climate, and place provided lasting influences on his work. With Princeton, New Jersey architect Jules Gregory, he designed a series of award-winning public schools and civic projects before moving to California in 1974. With architecture degrees from the University of Virginia and UCLA's School of Architecture and Urban Planning, John has also been active in teaching and research, leading graduate design studios at UCLA and Cornell University.

At UCLA he studied and associated with Charles Moore, joining Moore and Buzz Yudell in partnership in 1977.

Working closely with partner Buzz Yudell, John has helped to shape the firm's humanistic and inclusive approach to design, translating their deep concerns for human habitation and interaction into architecture and planning at many scales. As Principal-in-Charge his work has spanned many years of projects in Germany and Sweden, such as Tegel Harbor and the United States Embassy in Berlin, and Potatisåkern and Tango in Malmö. He has also found great satisfaction in the firm's long-term relationships with university campuses, such as University of California, Santa Cruz and the University of Washington's new campus in Tacoma. As Moore Ruble Yudell's portfolio has expanded into new areas of expertise—from laboratories to courthouses—John has sought to make each work part of a broad, sustained exploration in the creation of place.

Buzz Yudell, FAIA

Buzz Yudell's passion for architecture grew out of a synthesis of artistic and social concerns. At Yale College his work in sculpture was complemented by exploration of the sciences and humanities. Graduate study at Yale expanded these commitments to a range of scales from small constructions *in situ* to urban design. Here he began his long association with Charles Moore. In 1977, Buzz joined Charles and John Ruble in a partnership based on shared humanistic values and a celebration of collaboration within the office and beyond to their clients and communities.

Buzz has collaborated intensively with John to expand the firm's expression and expertise to campus, cultural, civic, and residential architecture. His commitment to creating humane places inspired by climatic and cultural understanding has informed the firm's work at many scales. Buzz continues to be as interested in the design and crafting of lighting and furniture as in planning for urban infill or sustainable growth.

His strong interest in the house as the quantum of community has helped to create a body of timeless residential work. As Principal-in-Charge, he has led projects in Asia, Europe, the Caribbean, and throughout the Unites States. His interest in nurturing community has found fresh expression on numerous campuses including UCLA, UCSB, Cal Tech, University of Cincinnati, Dartmouth, and MIT.

Throughout his career, teaching, research, writing, and community service have been critical to the evolution and exploration of both the theoretical and physical role of architecture in shaping and celebrating place and community.

Krista Becker, AIA

Krista Becker graduated Magna Cum Laude from the University of Southern California. She joined the firm in 2002, bringing extensive programming and space planning, design, and project management experience in large scale civic, commercial, health care, master-planning, museum, and retail projects. As project manager for the United States Embassy in Berlin, she is responsible for overall project management and works directly with the client to establish project goals and objectives. Krista is directly involved in the project organization and scheduling, and oversees the multidisciplinary consultant coordination, specifications, detailing, value analysis, project budget, programming through construction administration of a project. She is a Registered Architect in the State of California, and teaches at University California Los Angeles Extension in the Construction Management Certificate Program.

Jeanne Chen, AIA

Jeanne Chen earned both a BS and a Masters of Architecture from the University of Illinois, Champaign-Urbana, and joined the firm in 1989. As project manager, Jeanne combines design sensitivity with skills in technical coordination throughout the design process from the earliest program phases through documents and construction. At Moore Ruble Yudell, she has shown an affinity for large scale projects involving multiple user groups and complex program requirements. Jeanne's ability to advance and develop the broad vision of each project while attending to client needs and technical detail has made her successful in leading complex institutional and civic projects, including major renovations and additions, such as the Hugh & Hazel Darling Law Library Addition at UCLA. As Associate-in-Charge, her recent work includes master planning and design of academic and student housing projects for Dartmouth College in Hanover, New Hampshire. Since 1998, Jeanne has directed Moore Ruble Yudell's team throughout the design and construction of the firm's largest civic project, the United States Federal Building and Courthouse in Fresno, California. Jeanne is a Registered Architect in the State of California.

Michael de Villiers, AIA

Michael de Villiers received his B.Arch at the University of Cape Town, South Africa. After graduating, he worked on several commercial and housing projects in Cape Town. He obtained his M.Arch at the University of California, Los Angeles and joined Moore Ruble Yudell in 1987. Michael has extensive experience on large complex projects, including considerable university project experience at the University of California, San Diego, UCLA, and the University of Washington. As Project Manager and Associate-in-Charge, he has led all phases of project development on projects with full architectural services from pre-design through construction, on building types including libraries and science laboratories. At the UCLA Powell Library, he worked on issues of seismic and historical renovation, and at the University of Washington Tacoma campus, on issues of adaptive reuse and new building in historic contexts. His interest and experience in housing issues at all scales includes master planning, the development of typologies, and building design in projects ranging from low- to high-rise in California and Sydney, Australia. His projects include the new Santa Monica Public Library and a residential tower in San Francisco. Michael is a Registered Architect in the State of California.

Michael S. Martin, AIA

Michael Martin graduated with honors from the University of Illinois, Champaign-Urbana in 1976. As Principal Partner with The Aspen Design Group from 1981 to 1985, he focused on developing sustainable architecture including the headquarters for The Rocky Mountain Institute. During his six years in New York, he designed and managed projects for Peter Gluck and Partners and Kohn Pederson Fox and Associates. Projects accomplished with KPF included Canary Wharf FC-6 in London and the World Bank Headquarters in Washington, D.C.

After earning a Masters of Architecture II degree from the UCLA School of Architecture and Urban Planning in 1993, Michael established his own firm in Los Angeles. He joined Moore Ruble Yudell in 1997, and soon became Associate-in-Charge of number of large-scale academic and institutional projects. Selected projects include the Physical Sciences Building at UC Santa Cruz; Manzanita Village, a new 800-bed student housing campus at UC Santa Barbara; and The Science Center at Duke University, a complex of new and renovated facilities for five science departments. He has also guided the completion of three new buildings—an administration building, cafeteria, and laboratory facility—at Amgen Corporation's Longmont Colorado manufacturing center.

Neal Matsuno, AIA

Neal Matsuno joined the firm shortly after graduating from the University of Southern California in 1984. As a project manager, Neal combines design sensitivity with skills in technical coordination throughout the design process. His areas of special expertise include architectural lighting design. Neal has had a major responsibility for lighting design and technical detailing for projects including the California Center for the Arts in Escondido, Powell Library and Darling Law Library at the University of California, Los Angeles, as well as the firm's residential projects. As Associate-in-Charge he has led teams on a broad spectrum of projects such as the East Campus Master Plan and MIT Sloan School of Management/SHASS/Dewey Library project at the Massachusetts Institute of Technology; Glorya Kaufman Hall World Arts and Cultures Center at UCLA; the Cayman Island Town Master Plan, Grand Cayman; the Walt Disney Imagineering Campus Master Plan, Glendale, California; and the National Tropical Botanical Gardens Library and Herbarium, Kauai, Hawaii.

Neal is a Registered Architect in the State of California and has won numerous lighting design awards for his work on the California Center for the Arts in Escondido including: the IIDA Edwin F. Guth Memorial Award of Excellence for Interior Lighting Design, the Lumen West Award for Lighting Design, and the GE Edison Award of Excellence.

James Mary O'Connor

Born in Dublin, Ireland, James Mary O'Connor came to Charles Moore's Master Studios at UCLA in 1982 as a Fulbright Scholar James received his Bachelor of Science in Architecture degree from Trinity College Dublin, his Diploma in Architecture from the Dublin Institute of Technology, and his Master of Architecture from UCLA.

As Associate-in-Charge, James has provided spirited design and project management for residential, academic and mixed-use urban projects, including: Kobe Nishiokamoto Housing in Japan, the Horace Mann Elementary School and Fairmont Towers Hotel Addition, both in San Jose, California. International work has become a focus, with large-scale housing and planning projects such as the Potatisåkern and Tango projects in Malmö, Sweden, mixed-use development Project Yoda in Manila, and Tianjin-Xinhe New Town in Tianjin, People's Republic of China. His interest in uncommon building types is reflected in the Sunlaw Power Plant Prototype in Los Angeles, and the Santa Monica Civic Center Parking Structure. With irrepressible energy, James has also led Moore Ruble Yudell teams in national and international design competitions, such as the Beijing Wanhao Century Center, and the winning design for the Clarice Smith Performing Arts Center in College Park, Maryland.

Over the past 15 years, James has taught design studio, lectured, and has been invited as guest critic at UCLA, USC, SCI-Arc, the University of Calgary, Alberta and the University of Hawaii, Manoa.

Mario Violich

With a background in landscape architecture and architecture, Mario Violich's professional and academic experiences blur the traditional boundaries between building and landscape. After completing a Bachelor of Landscape Architecture at the University of California, Berkeley, Mario worked in landscape architecture and planning for the SWA Group in Sausalito and Laguna Beach. He later attended the University of California, Los Angeles, receiving a Masters of Architecture degree in 1989. Mario joined Moore Ruble Yudell the same year.

With a design approach that blends conceptual clarity and profound intuition, Mario has collaborated on a broad spectrum of projects ranging from master planning to institutional buildings, to residential gardens and houses. His work as Associate-in Charge includes: the Student Life Center at the University of Cincinnati, Ohio; The National Tropical Botanical Garden (master plan and library) in Kauai, Hawaii; Temple Beth-El Synagogue, Berkeley, California; Ruddell Residence, Kauai; Wasserstein Residence, Santa Barbara, California; and the Falkenberg Residence in Woodside, California and the Livermore Residence, in Carmel, California.

Mario is a member of the American Society of Landscape Architects, has been an instructor at the Department of Landscape Architecture at UCLA Extension since 1993, and an associate teacher at UCLA and UC Berkeley.

Tina Beebe

Tina Beebe received her MFA from the Yale School of Art and Architecture. Working with Charles Moore as a student, Tina joined his firm in Essex, Connecticut and subsequently came to California to work with him in 1976. She also worked in the office of Charles and Ray Eames, learning much from her great friend and mentor, Ray Eames. As resident colorist and interior designer for Moore Ruble Yudell, Tina has integrated these influences with her extensive travel experiences to inform her choices for custom color and material palettes on commercial, institutional, and residential projects. She has provided consulting services for many distinguished architecture firms in the United States and abroad.

Tina's practice has expanded to combine her design and color abilities to include the design of gardens for residential and commercial settings. As plant material inspires her color palette, color evokes ideas for whole gardens, which in turn complement and enhance the color and materials of architecture. This unique approach is exemplified in her color and landscape design for the award-winning Tango Housing at the Bo01 Exhibition in Malmö, Sweden. Tina has successfully applied principles of color and landscape at an extraordinary range of scales, from her own houses and gardens in Malibu and Sea Ranch, California, to the coloring of whole townscapes at Karow-Nord, Berlin, and Tianjin, China.

Below, seated, left to right:
James Mary O'Connor, John Ruble, Tina Beebe, Jeanne Chen.
standing, left to right:
Krista Becker, Neal Matsuno, Michael S. Martin, Buzz Yudell, Michael de Villiers, Mario Violich

project chronology

1977-1979
Rodes House,
Los Angeles, California

1979-1983
St. Matthew's Episcopal Church,
Pacific Palisades, California

1980-1985
Kwee House,
Singapore

1981-1983
Marine Street House,
Santa Monica, California

1981-1988
Tegel Harbor Phase I Housing,
Berlin, Germany

1982
Parador Hotel,
San Juan Capistrano, California
(project)

1982-1989
San Antonio Art Institute,
San Antonio, Texas

1983 competition
Center for Integrated Systems,
Stanford University, California

1983-1987
Saint Louis Art Museum,
West Wing Renovation and
new Decorative Arts Galleries,
Saint Louis, Missouri

1983-1989
Plaza Las Fuentes Mixed-use
Development,
Phase I and II,
Pasadena, California

1984-1987
Inman House,
Atlanta, Georgia

1984-1988
Humboldt Bibliothek,
Berlin, Germany

1984-1993
Bel Air Presbyterian Church,
Los Angeles, California

1984 competition; 1984-1987
Carousel Park,
Santa Monica Pier, California

1985-1988
Anawalt House,
Malibu, California

1985-1989
Church of the Nativity,
Rancho Santa Fe, California

1985-1989
University of Oregon Science Complex
Master Plan,
Eugene, Oregon

1986-1988
Peter Boxenbaum Arts Education Centre,
Crossroads School,
Santa Monica, California

1986-1989
First Church of Christ Scientist,
Glendale, California

1986-1995
UCSD Cellular and Molecular Medicine,
East and West Wings, Phase I & II,
University of California, San Diego

1987-1989
Walter A. Haas School of Business,
University of California, Berkeley

1987-1989
Yudell/Beebe House,
Malibu, California

1987-1994
California Center for the Arts,
Escondido, California

1988
Klingelhofer Diplomat Housing and Mixed-Use,
Berlin, Germany

1988-1995
Chemistry Building,
University of Washington, Seattle

1988-1996
Nishiokamoto Housing,
Phase I and II,
Kobe, Japan

1988-1996
Powell Library Seismic Renovation,
University of California, Los Angeles

1988-2002
Potatisåkern Housing and Villas,
Phase I & II; Phase III,
Malmö, Sweden

1990 competition
Bolle Center,
Berlin, Germany

1990-1993
Villa Superba,
Venice, California

1991 competition
Friedrichstadt Passagen,
Berlin, Germany

1991-1994
Schetter House,
Pacific Palisades, California

1991-1998
Berliner Strasse Housing,
Potsdam, Germany

1991-2003
Tacoma Campus Master Plan,
Phase I and II completion,
University of Washington, Tacoma

1992-1995
Dong-Hwa National University
Master Plan Phase I,
Hwa-Lien, Taiwan

1992 competition; 1992-1994
Peek & Cloppenburg Department Store,
Leipzig, Germany

1992 competition; 1992-1996
Avery House,
California Institute of Technology,
Pasadena, California

1992 competition; 1992-1999
Karow-Nord Housing,
Berlin-Weissensee, Germany

1992 competition; 1993-1998
Kirchsteigfeld Housing,
Potsdam, Germany

1992-1994
Walrod House,
Berkeley, California

1992-1998
Hugh & Hazel Darling
Law Library Addition,
University of California, Los Angeles

1993 competition
Kao-Shiung National Institute of
Technology Campus Master Plan,
Taiwan

1993 competition
Lewis & Clark College Master Plan
and Student Center,
Portland, Oregon

1993-1996 competition
Konstancin Housing,
Warsaw, Poland

1993-2000
Göttingen Master Plan,
Bahnhof Westseite, Germany

1993-1998
Sherman M. Fairchild Library of
Engineering and Applied Science,
California Institute of Technology,
Pasadena, California

1994 competition; 1994-2001
Clarice Smith Performing Arts Center,
University of Maryland, College Park

1994-1995
Playa Vista Office Campus Study,
Los Angeles, California (project)

1994-2003
Wasserstein House,
Santa Barbara, California

1995 competition
Stanford University Graduate School of
Business Residential Learning Center,
Palo Alto, California

1995-1997
Kartanes Winter Resort Hotel,
Uludag, Turkey

1995-1998
Percival/Westbrook House,
Newport Beach, California

1995-1999
Shmuger/Hamagami House,
Pacific Palisades, California

1995 competition; 1996-in progress
United States Embassy,
Berlin, Germany

1996-1997
Mustique House,
French Virgin Islands (project)

1996-1997
Yorkin House,
Malibu, California

1996-1998
Elizabeth Moore House,
Orinda, California

1996-1998
Gilbert House Remodel,
Los Angeles, California

1996-1999
Graalfs House,
Berlin, Germany

1996-1999
Tiergarten Dreieck,
Berlin, Germany

1996-2002
Regatta Wharf at Jackson's Landing,
Phase I and II,
Pyrmont, Sydney, Australia

1996-in progress
New Town Master Plan,
Grand Cayman, Cayman Islands

1996-in progress
United States Courthouse and
Federal Building,
Fresno, California

1996, 2002-in progress
Tulane Housing,
Louisiana

1997-1998
Miramar Villas,
Istanbul, Turkey

1997-1998
Nautilus Residences,
Yesilyurt, Turkey

1997-1999
Baas/Walrod House,
The Sea Ranch, California

1997-1999
Göttingen Office Building,
Göttingen, Germany

1997-2001
Yudell/Beebe House,
The Sea Ranch, California

1997-2002
Fairmont Towers Hotel Addition,
San Jose, California

1997-2002
Interdisciplinary Sciences Building,
University of California, Santa Cruz

1997-2002
Manzanita Village,
University of California, Santa Barbara

1997-in progress
Congregation Beth El,
Berkeley, California

1998
House for the Next Millennium,
House Beautiful magazine (project)

1998-2000
Disney Imagineering GC3 Master Plan,
Glendale, California

1998-2003
Horace Mann Elementary School,
San Jose, California

1998-in progress
MIT Sloan School of Management/
SHASS/Dewey Library
Massachusetts Institute of Technology,
Cambridge

1998-in progress
Russell Tutt Science Building,
Colorado College, Colorado Springs

1998-2002
Physical Sciences Building,
University of California, Santa Cruz

1999-2001
Tango,
Bo01 Housing Exhibition,
Malmö, Sweden

1999-2002
New Science Building,
University of Washington, Tacoma
Tacoma, Washington

1999-in progress
The Falkenberg Residence,
Woodside, California

1999-in progress
Student Life Center,
University of Cincinnati, Ohio

1999-in progress
Glorya Kaufman Hall,
Center for World Arts and Cultures,
University of California, Los Angeles

2000-2003
Halprin House,
The Sea Ranch, California

2000-in progress
Bryant Street Seawall Condominiums,
San Francisco

2001-2002
Inclusion Area D Faculty Housing
Master Plan,
University of California, Santa Cruz

2001-in progress
606 Broadway,
Santa Monica, California

2001-in progress
Amgen Laboratories and Administration Building,
Longmont, Colorado

2001-in progress
Dartmouth College North Campus
Master Plan, Kemeny Hall & Center for
Humanities, Student Housing, and
Dining & Social Commons,
Hanover, New Hampshire

2001-in progress
Santa Monica Public Parking Structure,
Santa Monica, California

2001-in progress
The Livermore Residence,
Carmel, California

2002 competition
Beijing Century Center,
Beijing, People's Republic of China

2002 competition
United States Air Force Memorial,
Arlington, Virginia

2003-in progress
The Science Center,
Duke University,
Durham, North Carolina

2002-in progress
Project Yoda,
Fort Bonicafio City,
Manila, Philippines

2002-in progress
Santa Monica Main Library
Santa Monica, California

2002-in progress
The Ruddell House,
Kauai, Hawaii

2003-in progress
Tianjin Xin-he Housing,
Tianjin, People's Republic of China

2002-in progress
Western Asset Plaza,
Pasadena, California

2003-in progress
Natural Sciences Building
St. Edward's University
Austin, Texas

project credits

Tacoma Campus Master Plan
University of Washington, Tacoma

Client: University Architects/Capital Projects
Office, University of Washington
Design Architect: Moore Ruble Yudell
Architects & Planners
Principal-in-Charge: John Ruble
Principal: Buzz Yudell
Associates-in-charge: Stephen Harby, Michael
de Villiers
Color and Materials: Tina Beebe
Project Manager: Steve Gardner
Project team: Gene Treadwell, Richard Williams,
Tony Reyes, Oli Florendo, Chris Kenney, Erica
Moon, David Kaplan, Neal Matsuno, Angel
Gabriel, Ric Tayag, Wendy Kohn, Tony Tran,
Adrian Koffka, Rebecca Bubenas, Ed Diamante
Model makers: Mark Grand, Florence Huang,
Tony Pritchard
Renderer: Al Forster
Photographer: Werner Huthmacher

Executive Architect: LMN Architects
Principal-in-Charge: John Nesholm
Project managers: Rich Wilson, Jim Cade

Landscape Architects: Hanna/Olin, Ltd., Jones
& Jones
Principal-in-Charge: Robert Hanna
Principal-in-Charge: Ilza Jones

Tiergarten Dreieck
Berlin, Germany

Client: Groth + Graalfs Industrie und Wohnbau
GmbH
Design Architect: Moore Ruble Yudell
Architects & Planners
Principal-in-Charge: John Ruble
Principal: Buzz Yudell
Project Architect: Adrian Koffka
Project team: Christian Daniels, Mark Grand,
Christopher Hamilton, Erin Hillhouse,
Adam Padua
Photographer: Werner Huthmacher

Associate Architect: Lunetto & Fischer, Berlin

Landscape Architect: Lützow 7
Principals: Cornelia Müller, Jan Wehberg

The Peg Yorkin House
Malibu, California

Client: Peg Yorkin, David Yorkin, and Nicole
Yorkin
Design Architect: Moore Ruble Yudell
Architects & Planners
Principal-in-Charge: Buzz Yudell
Principal: John Ruble
Associate-in-Charge: Marc Schoeplein
Color and Materials: Tina Beebe
Lighting: Neal Matsuno
Landscape: Tina Beebe, Mario Violich
Project team: Tim Eng, Ed Diamante, Bob
Anderson, Don Aitken, Scott Walter, Michael
Martin, Mariana Boctor, Steve Penhoet,
Christian Daniels
Model makers: Mark Grand, Ken Pai
Photographer: Kim Zwarts

Dartmouth College North Campus Master Plan
Hanover, New Hampshire
Client: Dartmouth College

Competition and Project Credits
Design Architect: Moore Ruble Yudell
Architects & Planners
Principal-in-Charge: Buzz Yudell
Principal: John Ruble
Associate-in-Charge: Jeanne Chen
Competition team: Bob Dolbinski, Ross
Morishige, Kaoru Orime
Model makers: Mark Grand, Alex Solbes, Donald
Hornbeck
Renderers: James Mary O'Connor, Tony Tran

Project Architect: Bob Dolbinski
Color and Materials: Tina Beebe, Yana
Khudyakova, Kaoru Orime
Project team: Chris Bach, Matt Blake, Laurie
Groehler, Neal Matsuno, Wing-Hon Ng, Chris
Hamilton, Kyung-Sun Lee, Ross Morishige, Mar-
tin Saavedra, Matt Vincent
Model makers: Mark Grand, Gerardo Rivero,
Joan Young

Associate Architect: Bruner/Cott & Associates
Principal-in-Charge: Leland Cott
Principal, Project Manager: Lynne Brooks
Project team: Dan Raih, Kevin Deabler, Anne-
Sophie Divenyi, Shaun Dempsey, Martina
Johnson, Jason Springer, Jason Forney

Landscape Architect: Richard Burck Associates
Graphic Design: Strong Cohen
Principal: Tom Strong

Physical Sciences Building
University of California, Santa Cruz

Client: Office of Physical Planning and Construction, UC Santa Cruz
Design Architect: Moore Ruble Yudell Architects & Planners
Principal-in-Charge: John Ruble
Principal: Buzz Yudell
Associate-in-Charge: Michael Martin
Color and Materials: Tina Beebe
Project managers: Erin Hillhouse, Wing-Hon Ng
Project team: Murat Sanal, Ada Mancilla, Alberto Reano
Model makers: Mark Grand, Matthew Vincent, Vely Zajec
Renderer: Al Forster
Digital illustration: Ross Morishige, Oliver Matla
Photographer: Werner Huthmacher
Model Photographer: Jim Simmons

Executive Architect: Anshen + Allen, San Francisco
Principal-in-Charge: Gregory Blackburn
Associate Principal: Marissa Tweedie

Project Architect: Herb Moussa

Landscape: Joni L. Janecki & Associates
Principal-in-Charge: Joni L. Janecki

Laboratory Consultant: Research Facilities Design

Interdisciplinary Sciences Building
University of California, Santa Cruz

Client: Office of Physical Planning and Construction, UC Santa Cruz
Design Architect: Moore Ruble Yudell Architects & Planners
Principal-in-Charge: John Ruble
Principal: Buzz Yudell
Color and Materials: Kaoru Orime
Project Manager: Wing-Hon Ng
Project team: Adrian Koffka, Doug Pierson, Miguel San Miguel, Katherine Yi
Photographer: Werner Huthmacher
Model Photographer: Jim Simmons

Executive Architect: EHDD

Principal-in-Charge: Charles Davis
Landscape Architect: Pamela Burton & Co.

East Campus Master Plan
MIT Sloan School of Management, Massachusetts Institute of Technology, Cambridge

Client: Massachusetts Institute of Technology
Design Architect: Moore Ruble Yudell Architects & Planners
Principal-in-Charge: Buzz Yudell
Principal: John Ruble
Associate-in-Charge: Neal Matsuno
Color and materials: Tina Beebe, Kaoru Orime
Project team: Matthew Blake, Ross Morishige, Kaoru Orime, JT Theeuwes
Model makers: Mark Grand, Zachary Benedict
Renderer: Al Forster

Associate Architect: Sasaki Associates
Principal-in-Charge: Norris Strawbridge
Associate-in-Charge: Will Gerstmyer

Landscape: Olin Partnership
Principal-in-Charge: Laurie D. Olin
Associate-in-Charge: David Rubin

Clarice Smith Performing Arts Center
University of Maryland, College Park

Client: Engineering and Architectural Services, University of Maryland

Competition and Project credits
Design Architect: Moore Ruble Yudell Architects & Planners
Principal-in-Charge: Buzz Yudell
Principal: John Ruble
Associates-in-charge: Jim Morton, James Mary O'Connor
Color and Materials: Tina Beebe
Project managers: Hong Chen, Denise Haradem, Martin Saavedra
Competition Team: Celina Welch, Bob Anderson, Erica Moon, Daniel Garness, Shuji Kurokawa, Akai Ming-Kae Yang, Mark Peacor, Tony Tran, Mario Violich, Adrian Koffka, Adam Padua
Project team: Harry Steinway, Mary Jane Kopitzke, Alfeo B. Diaz, Erica Moon, Bob Anderson, Adam Padua, Kaz Baba, Wendy Kohn, Akai Ming-Kae Yang, Richard Williams, Amy Alper, Holly Bieniewski, Michael Xu, Christine Cho, Thurman Grant, Mary Beth Elliott, Sara Loe, Angel Gabriel, Will Shepphird, Tony Tran
Model makers: Mark Grand, Chris Roades, Craig Currie
Photographers: Werner Huthmacher, Alan Karchmer, Jim Simmons
Renderers: Al Forster, Daniel Garness

Associate Architect: Ayers/Saint/Gross Architects
Principal-in-Charge: Richard Ayers
Project team: Adam Gross, George Thomas, Duncan Kirk, John Dale, Peter Garver

Landscape Architect: Michael Vergason Landscape

Theater Consultants: Theater Projects Consultants, Inc

Acoustical Consultants: R Lawrence Kirkegaard & Associates

Interior Furnishings: Audrey Alberts Design

Lighting: David A. Mintz

Shmuger/Hamagami House
Pacific Palisades, California

Client: Marc Shmuger and Louise Hamagami
Design Architect: Moore Ruble Yudell Architects & Planners
Principal-in-Charge: Buzz Yudell
Principal: John Ruble
Associate-in-Charge: Marc Schoeplein
Color and Materials: Tina Beebe
Project team: Bob Anderson, Ed Diamante, Tim Eng, Neal Matsuno, Mario Violich
Model makers: Mark Grand, Laurian Pokroy, Tim Eng, David Ellien
Photographer: Tim Hursley

Landscape Architect: Jay Griffith, Landscapes Inc

Interior Furnishings: Audrey Alberts Design

United States Courthouse and Federal Building
Fresno, California

Client: General Services Administration
Design Architect: Moore Ruble Yudell Architects & Planners
Principal-in-Charge: John Ruble
Principal: Buzz Yudell
Associate-in-Charge: Jeanne Chen
Project Architect: Bob Dolbinski
Colors and materials: Tina Beebe, Kaoru Orime
Project team: Chris Hamilton, Tim Eng, Ross Morishige, Roger Lopez, Tony Tran
Models: Mark Grand, Vely Zajec, Joshua Lunn, Matthew Vincent
Renderer: Doug Jamieson
Digital Illustration: Ross Morishige

Executive Architect: Gruen Associates
Principal-in-Charge: Debra Gerod

Landscape Architect: Pamela Burton & Co.

Interiors: Brayton & Hughes Design Studio

Lighting: Frances Krahe & Associates

Santa Monica Public Library
Santa Monica, California

Client: City of Santa Monica
Architect: Moore Ruble Yudell
Principal-in-Charge: John Ruble
Principal: Buzz Yudell
Associates-in-charge: Krista Becker; Michael de Villiers
Colors and materials: Tina Beebe, Kaoru Orime, Yana Khudyakova
Project team: Richard Destin, Krista Scheib, Haekwan Park, Clay Holden, Bob Dolbinski, Angel Gabriel, Roger Lopez, Oscar Pineda, Martin Saavedra, Neal Matsuno, Scott Allen, Gerlinde Arztmann, Simone Barth, Mark Bittoni, Chad Christopher, Ed Diamante, Tim Feigenbutz, Bernardo Frias, Benjamin Gramann, Laurie Groehler, Konrad Hrehorowicz, Ted Kane, Therese Kelly, Henry Lau, Sun Lee, Frank Maldonado, Alberto Reano, Gerardo Rivero, Carissa Shrock, Alex Solbes, Isabel Stomm, JT Theeuwes, Tony Tran, Kim Valino, Matt Vincent, Joan Young, Vely Zajec
Model makers: Mark Grand, John Leimbach, Zachary Benedict
Model Photographer: Jim Simmons
Digital illustrations: Craig Shimahara Illustration, Ross Morishige, Halil Dolan, Harayuki Yokoyama

Interior Furnishings: CNI Design

Lighting: Patrick Quigley & Associates

Beijing Wanhao Century Center
Beijing, People's Republic of China

Design Architect: Moore Ruble Yudell
Architects & Planners
Principal-in-Charge: John Ruble
Principal: Buzz Yudell
Associate-in-Charge: James Mary O'Connor
Color and materials: Tina Beebe, Kaoru Orime
Project team: Halil Dolan, Tony Tran, Alberto
Reano, Angel Gabriel, Bill Ferehawk, Isabel
Stomm, Kaoru Orime, Vely Zajec, Yana
Khudyakova, Ed Diamante, Richard Destin,
Chris Hamilton, Kyung-Sun Lee
Models makers: Mark Grand, Alex Solbes,
Haruyuki Yokoyama
Research: Rebecca Bubenas, Janet Sager
Digital Illustrator: Craig Shimahara Illustration
Presentation Model: Model Concepts
Model Photographer: Jim Simmons

Associate Architect: Yang Architects
Principal-in-Charge: Akai Ming-Kae Yang

United States Air Force Memorial (project)
Arlington, Virginia

Client: United States Air Force
Competition: May 2002
Design Architect: Moore Ruble Yudell
Architects & Planners
Principal-in-Charge: Buzz Yudell
Principal: John Ruble
Associate-in-Charge: Mario Violich
Color and materials: Tina Beebe, Yana
Khudyakova
Project Team: Halil Dolan, Ross Morishige
Model makers: Mark Grand, Halil Dolan
Research and graphics: Halil Dolan, Ross
Morishige, Rebecca Bubenas, Janet Sager
Model Photographer: Jim Simmons

Structural Engineering: Arup San Francisco
Cost Consulting: Davis Langdon Adamson

Potatisåkern Housing
Malmö, Sweden

Client: Skanska Nya Hem, Phase I & II; HSB
Malmö, Phase III; MKB Fastighets AB, Phase IV
Design Architect: Moore Ruble Yudell
Architects & Planners
Principal-in-Charge: John Ruble
Principals: Buzz Yudell, Charles Moore
Associates-in-Charge:
Phases II, III and IV: James Mary O'Connor
Phase I: Cecily Young
Concept Phase: Renzo Zecchetto
Color and Materials: Tina Beebe
Project team:
Phases II, III and IV: Lisa Belian, Izzet Motola,
Adam Padua, Tony Tran, Roger Lopez, Erin
Hillhouse, Ken Kim, Alberto Reano
Phase I: Ying-Chao Kuo, Chris Duncan, Tea
Sapo, Yeon Keun Jeong, Mary Beth Elliott,
Steven Gardner, John Taft, Tony Tran, James
Mary O'Connor, Wing-Hon Ng
Landscape Design: John Ruble, Cecily Young,
James Mary O'Connor, Tina Beebe
Model makers: Mark Grand, Craig Currie,
Matthew Vincent, Dirk Schoerner
Renderer: George Nakatani
Photographer: Werner Huthmacher, Lars
Finnström, Lars Mong

Associate & Executive Architect:
Phase I and II: SWECO/FFNS Arkitekter, Malmö
with Hultin & Lundquist Arkitekter
SWECO/FFNS
Principal-in-Charge: Bertil Öhrström,
Project Manager: Lars Lindahl
Hultin & Lundquist:
Principal-in-Charge: Kurt Hultin
Project Manager: Dennis Johnsson
Phase II (Villas): Hultin & Lundquist
Arkitekter AB
Principal-in-Charge: Kurt Hultin
Project Manager: Dennis Johnsson
Phase III (HSB Building):
Mernsten Arkitektkontor AB
Principal-in-Charge: Bertil Mernsten
Hultin & Lundquist Arkitekter AB
Principals: Kurt Hultin, Dennis Johnsson
Phase IV: SWECO/FFNS Arkitekter AB
Principal-in-Charge: Bertil Öhrström,
Project Manager: Lars Lindahl
Project team: Maria Listrup, Cecilia Spannel,
Bengt-Åke Jarnestad, Charlotta Rosén

Executive Landscape Architect: PRMarkDesign
Principal-in-Charge: Per Renwart

United States Embassy
Berlin, Germany

Client: United States Department of State

Competition and Project Credits
Design Architect: Moore Ruble Yudell
Architects & Planners
Principal-in-Charge: John Ruble
Principal: Buzz Yudell
Competition Project Manager: Cecily Young
Color & Materials: Tina Beebe
Competition team: Richard Destin,
Adrian Koffka, Marc Schoeplein, Will Sheppird,
Gene Treadwell
Project Associate-in-Charge: Krista Becker
Design Manager: Adam Padua
Color & Materials: Tina Beebe, Kaoru Orime,
Yana Khudyakova
Project team: Bernardo Frias, JT Theeuwes,
Oscar Pineda, Michael Martin, Jerome Chang,
Therese Kelly, Tiffany Pang, Joan Young, Chris
Hamilton, Matt Blake, Matt Vincent, Vely Zajec,
Adrian Koffka, Chris Bach, Tim Feigenbutz,
Therese Kelly, Tony Tran
Model makers: Mark Grand, Veronica Vela,
John Leimbach, Zachary Benedict
Presentation Model: Model Concepts, Inc.
Photographer: Del Zoppo/Simmons
Renderer: Doug Jamieson

Associate Technical Architect: Gruen Associates
Landscape: Olin Partnership
Interiors: Brayton & Hughes Design Studio
Lighting: Horton Lees Brogden Lighting Design
Graphics: Sussman/Prejza & Company, Inc.

Baas/Walrod House
The Sea Ranch, California

Client: Jacqueline Baas, Steven Walrod
Architect: Moore Ruble Yudell
Architects & Planners
Principal-in-Charge: Buzz Yudell
Principal: John Ruble
Associate-in-Charge: Marc Schoeplein
Color and Materials: Tina Beebe
Lighting: Neal Matsuno
Project team: Laurian Pokroy, Tim Eng, Scott
Walter, Ada Mancilla, Martin Saavedra
Model Maker: Mark Grand
Photographer: Kim Zwarts, Marc Schoeplein

Tango
Malmö, Sweden

Client: MKB Fastighets AB
Design Architect: Moore Ruble Yudell
Architects & Planners with FFNS Architects
Principal-in-Charge: John Ruble
Principal: Buzz Yudell
Associate-in-Charge: James Mary O'Connor
Color and materials: Tina Beebe, Kaoru Orime
Interior Design, Exhibition Apartment:
Tina Beebe, Kaoru Orime
Project team: Lisa Belian, Tony Tran
Landscape design: John Ruble, James Mary
O'Connor, Tina Beebe, Kaoru Orime
Model makers: Mark Grand, Chad T. Takenaka,
Vely Zajec, Don Hornbeck, Joshua Lunn,
Matthew Vincent, Lance Collins
Renderer, Digital Renderings: Ross Morishige
Photographer: Werner Huthmacher, Ole Jais

Executive Architect: SWECO FFNS Architects
Principal: Bertil Öhrström
Project architects: Karin Bellander, Lars
Lindahl
Landscape Architect: Siv Degerman

Interior designers: Karin Bellander, Johanna
Wittenmark

Project management: SWECO Projektledning
AB
Project Manager: Pär Hammarberg
Assistant Project Manager and IT Coordinator:
Conny Nilsson

Yudell/Beebe House
The Sea Ranch, California

Client: Buzz Yudell and Tina Beebe
Architect: Moore Ruble Yudell
Architects & Planners
Principal-in-Charge: Buzz Yudell
Associate-in-Charge: Marc Schoeplein
Color and Materials: Tina Beebe
Landscape: Tina Beebe
Lighting: Buzz Yudell
Project team: Tim Eng, Scott Walter,
Ed Diamante
Model makers: Mark Grand, Matthew Vincent,
Michael O'Bryan
Watercolor site plan: Tina Beebe
Photographer: Tim Hursley, Kim Zwarts

Regatta Wharf at Jackson's Landing
Pyrmont, Sydney, Australia

Client: Lend Lease Development
Design Architect: Moore Ruble Yudell
Architects & Planners
Principal-in-Charge: John Ruble
Principal: Buzz Yudell
Associate-in-Charge: Michael deVilliers
Color and materials: Tina Beebe, Kaoru Orime
Project team Phase I: Erin Hillhouse, Alberto
Reano, Murat Sanal, Stephen Penhoet, Roger
Lopez, Tony Tran, David Ellien
Project team Phase II: Edgar Diamante, Roger
Lopez, Vely Zajec, Tony Tran, Ross Morishige
Model Maker: Mark Grand
Photographers: Werner Huthmacher
Renderers: Al Forster, Ian Espinoza
Associate Architect: Travis McEwen Group,
North Sydney, Australia

Student Life Center
University of Cincinnati, Ohio

Client: Campus Planning, University of
Cincinnati
Design Architect: Moore Ruble Yudell
Architects & Planners
Principal-in-Charge: Buzz Yudell
Principal: John Ruble
Associate-in-Charge: Mario Violich
Project Manager: Adam Padua
Color and materials: Tina Beebe, Kaoru Orime
Project team: Bob Dolbinski, Alberto Reano,
Ted Kane, Alexis Bennett , Ross Morishige
Model makers: Mark Grand, Don Hornbeck
Digital illustrations: Ross Morishige, Glaser
Associates

Associate Architect: Glaser Associates
Principal-in-Charge: Arthur A. Hupp
Principal: Michael J. Moose
Principal/Project Manager: Steve Haber
Project Architect: Scott Layman

Master Plan/Landscape Architect: Hargreaves
Associates
Design Director: George Hargreaves
Principals-in-Charge: Mary Margaret Jones,
Glenn Allen
Graphic Designer: Marcia Shortt

Hugh & Hazel Darling Law Library
University of California, Los Angeles

Client: UCLA Design & Construction/Capital
Programs
Design Architect: Moore Ruble Yudell
Architects & Planners
Principal-in-Charge: Buzz Yudell
Principal: John Ruble
Associate-in-Charge: Jeanne Chen, Stephen
Harby
Color and Materials: Tina Beebe
Project team: Don Aitken, Bob Anderson, Angel
Gabriel, Wing-Hon Ng, Adam Padua, Martin
Saavedra, Ric Tayag, Tony Tran, Gene Treadwell,
Akai Ming-Kae Yang
Lighting: Neal Matsuno
Model Maker: Mark Grand
Photographer: Timothy Hursley

Landscape Architect: Pamela Burton & Co.

Interiors Furnishings: Audrey Alberts Design

Horace Mann Elementary School
San Jose, California

Client: San Jose Unified School District
The Redevelopment Agency of the City of
San Jose
Design Architect: Moore Ruble Yudell
Architects & Planners
Principal-in-Charge: John Ruble
Principal: Buzz Yudell
Associate-in-Charge: James Mary O'Connor
Color and materials: Tina Beebe, Kaoru Orime
Project Manager: Adam Padua
Project team: Alberto Reano, Lisa Belian, Ed
Diamante, Roger Lopez, Martin Saavedra,
Tony Tran
Model makers: Mark Grand, Matthew Vincent,
Vely Zajec, Lance Collins
Renderer: Al Forster
Photographer: John Linden

Executive Architect: BFGC Architects
Planners Inc
Project Manager: David Cartnal
Landscape Architect: Pamela Burton & Co

Manzanita Village
University of California, Santa Barbara

Client: UCSB Design & Construction/Capital
Programs
Design Architect: Moore Ruble Yudell
Architects & Planners
Principal-in-Charge: Buzz Yudell
Principal: John Ruble
Associate-in-Charge: Michael Martin
Color and materials: Tina Beebe, Kaoru Orime
Lighting: Neal Matsuno
Project Manager: Richard Destin
Project team: Ed Diamante, Alberto Reano,
Ted Kane, Laurie Groehler, Oliver Matla, Steve
Penhoet, Kenneth Kim, Katherine Yi, Izzet
Motola, Murat Sanal, David Ellien
Model makers: Mark Grand, Donald Hornbeck,
Joshua Lunn, Vely Zajec, Michael O'Bryan, Dirk
Schoerner
Renderers: Al Forster, Tony Tran
Photographer: Werner Huthmacher

Executive Architect: DesignARC, Santa Barbara,
California
Principal-in-Charge: J. Michael Holliday
Project Manager: Bruce Bartlett

bibliography

Selected Books

Ruble, John. "Libraries/Learning Centers." In *Building Type Basics for College and University Facilities,* edited by David J. Neuman , New York: John Wiley & Sons, 2003

"Moore Ruble Yudell Architecture & Planning" Tasarim, March 2003, Special Issue 129

Gause, Jo Allen. *Great Planned Communities.* Washington, DC: Urban Land Institute, June 2002

Residential Spaces of the World, Volume 5. Melbourne: The Images Publishing Group, 2002

Yee, Roger. *Educational Environments.* New York: Visual Reference Publications, Inc., 2002

Slessor, Catherine. *See-Through Houses: Inspirational Homes and Features in Glass.* London/New York: Ryland Peters & Small, 2001

Crisp, Barbara. *Human Spaces.* Massachusetts: Rockport Publishers, Inc., 2001

Cyberspace: the World of Digital Architecture. Melbourne: The Images Publishing Group, 2001

Hardenbergh, Don and Todd S. Phillips, eds. *Retrospective of Courthouse Design 1991-2001,* 2001

Dutton, John A. *New American Urbanism: Reforming the Suburban Metropolis.* Milan: Skira, 2001

Trulove, James Grayson and Il Kim, eds. *New American House 3.* New York: Watson-Guptill Publications, 2001

Goslee Power, Nancy and Susan Heeger. *The Gardens of California: Four Centuries of Design from Mission to Modern.* Clarkson N. Potter, Inc., June 17, 2000

"Moore Ruble Yudell Architecture & Planning: Projects: Part 2, Campus & Community." *Tasarim,* January/February 2000, Special Issue 98

Koffka, Adrian and Wendy Kohn, eds. *Moore Ruble Yudell: Building in Berlin.* Melbourne: The Images Publishing Group, 1999

"Moore Ruble Yudell Architecture & Planning: Houses & Housing." *Tasarim,* December 1999, Special Issue 97

Langdon, Philip, *American Houses.* New York: Stewart Tabori & Chang, 1997

Riera Ojeda, Oscar, James Mary O'Connor, and Wendy Kohn. *Campus & Community: Moore Ruble Yudell Architecture and Planning.* Rockport Publishers, Inc., 1997

Riera Ojeda, Oscar, ed. *The New American House.* Whitney Library of Design, 1995

Riera Ojeda, Oscar and Lucas H. Guerra, eds. *Moore Ruble Yudell: Houses and Housing.* AIA Press, 1994

Ferguson, R. *Urban Revisions: Current Projects in the Public Realm.* MIT Press, August 1994.

Webb, Michael and J. Carter Brown. *Architects House Themselves: Breaking New Ground.* The Preservation Press, 1994

Sanoff, Henry. *School Design.* New York: Van Nostrand Reinhold, 1994

Steele, James. *Museum Builders.* Academy Editions/Ernst & Sohn, London, 1994

Toy, Maggie, ed. *World Cities: Los Angeles.* London: Academy Editions and Berlin: Ernst + Sohn, 1994

Steele, James, ed. *Moore Ruble Yudell.* Academy Editions, 1993

"Moore Ruble Yudell, 1979-1982." *Architecture and Urbanism (A+U),* Special Issue. August 1992

Johnson, Eugene J. *Charles Moore Buildings and Projects 1949-1986.* New York: Rizzoli, 1986

Street-Porter, Tim. *Freestyle.* New York: Stewart Tabori & Chang, 1986

Selected Periodicals

Greenway Consulting Group. *2004 Almanac of Architecture & Design,* 2004

Heeger, Susan. "Testing Ground: A garden is a laboratory for a California color expert." *Martha Stewart Living,* September 2003

Chirkov, Andrei. "Against the Background of Ocean Expanse." *Interior Digest* (Russia), July 2003

Barreneche, Raul. "It Takes Tech to Tango." *Popular Science,* May 2003

Russell, Beverly. "Ten Most Sensuous Spaces." *SFDC News,* 2002

Barreneche, Raul. "Off the Grid: Green (and Red, and Blue...)" *Dwell,* December 2002

Webb, Michael. "Buzz Yudell/Tina Beebe: connecting to the land and the light at Sea Ranch." *Architectural Digest,* Volume 59, Number 9, September 2002

Hutchins, Shelly D. and Melissa Worden. "The Big House Clinic: Case Study House Dodici Giardini." *Residential Architect,* Volume 6, Number 8, Sept-Oct 2002

Thornburg, Barbara and Susan Heeger. "The Green Rooms: The Contemporary Tent." *Los Angeles Times Magazine,* May 19, 2002

Newman, Morris. "Sustaining in Sweden." *LA Architect,* May 2002

Weathersby, William Jr. "Tango Building, Malmö, Sweden." *Architectural Record,* February 2002

Yudell, Buzz. "Housing Futures: Making Place or Marketing Product?" Volume 01.2: *arcCA*

Lotand, Johan. "Tre Sovrum, Tre Stilar." (Three bedrooms, three styles) *Plaza Interiör,* Number 8, August 2001

Hawthorne, Christopher. "Moore or Less." *Architecture,* May 2001

Tortorich, Mark. "Contra Costa Government Center: A California Competition Achieves Public Advocacy Through Public Participation." *Competitions,* Spring 2001

Stenler, Anita. "Bomässa kan inspirera." (Housing exhibition inspires) *Cementa,* March 2001

Zevon, Susan. "Inside Out." *House Beautiful,* August 2000

Webb, Michael. "LA Houses: Building on a Modernist Tradition." *A+U,* May 2000

"Tango Housing Complex." *Space (Korea),* 417 pp.120-125, July 2000

Taggart, Brian. "Library as Urban Placemaker." *Competitions,* Summer 2000

"American Institute of Architects 1999 Honors & Awards." *Architectural Record,* May 1999

"The Boom Goes On." *American Libraries,* April 1999

"The Twentieth Century." *Architectural Digest,* April 1999

"Berlin Ambition." *Wallpaper,* January 1999

"Mission: Possible." *German Life,* Feb/March 1999

Los Angeles Heritage Magazine, Issue 1, The Los Angeles Conservancy, January 1999

"L'albero della vita." (The tree of life) *Chiesa Oggi,* 1999

"Images That Motivate." *Places,* Winter 1998

"Designing the Campus as a Community." *Planning for Higher Education,* Spring 1998

"Los Angeles: opération Playa Vista décollage différé." *Diagonal,* July-Aug 1998

"Houses for the Next Millennium." *House Beautiful,* October 1998

American Institute of Architects 1998 Honors & Awards. *Architectural Record,* May 1998

"Big Thinker for Pyrmont." *Sydney Morning Herald,* April 6, 1998

"Moore Ruble Yudell Architecture & Planning: Campus & Community." *Interni,* September 1997

"Moore Ruble Yudell–A Choreography of Community." *Dialogue,* September 1997

"By the Book." *Architecture,* March 1997

"The AD 100." *Architectural Digest,* September 1995

Weathersby, William Jr. "California Theatres: California Center for the Arts Escondido." *TCI,* January 1995

"Arts Fusion." *Architecture,* December 1994.

"Moore Ruble Yudell: Maryland Center for Performing Arts, Nativity Catholic Church." *KA* (Korean Architects), December 1994

"Moore Ruble Yudell: A Firm on the Go." *The World & I,* July 1994

"Earthly Delights, a California Design Couple's Country Idyll." *House Beautiful,* August 1992

"Outdoor Rooms." *Elle Decor,* April/May 1992

"University of Oregon Science Complex." *Architecture,* March/April 1992

"Nishiokamoto Housing." *Architecture,* January/February 1992

"Designers of the Year." *Interiors,* January 1992

"University of Oregon Science Complex." *Architectural Record,* November 1991

"1991–1992 Western Home Awards Award of Merit." *Sunset Magazine,* October 1991

Builder, June 1991

Tegel Harbor Housing. *Architecture,* May/June 1991

"Humboldt Bibliotek." *American Libraries,* April 1991

"Collaborative Genius", "Angeleno Gothic", "Campus Medicine." *Architecture,* March 1991

"Malibu on their Minds." *House and Garden,* February 1991

"Bel Air Presbyterian Church." *American Organist,* February 1991

"University of Oregon Science Complex." *Places,* Volume 7, Number 4, 1991

"Nativity Catholic Church." *Architectural Record,* February 1991

"Moore Ruble Yudell–A Malibu Residence." *Architectural Digest,* February 1990

"Pride of Place." *Architectural Record,* January 1990

"Berlino 1988." *Abitare,* May 1988

"Waterfront Housing at Once Exuberant and Classical." *Architecture,* May 1988

"Living by the Water." *Progressive Architecture,* October 1987

"Moore Ruble Yudell–Remodeling a Spanish Colonial House in Beverly Hills." *Architectural Digest,* September 1987

"Charles Moore." *Interiors,* September 1987

"Rebuilding Berlin, Yet Again." *Time,* June 1987

"Perfection in Miniature." *House Beautiful,* February 1987

"Overview of Recent Works." *Space Design,* November 1986

"Erste Projekte." (First projects) Berlin: Internationale Bauausstellung Berlin, 1984

"A Church is Not a Home." Newsweek, March 1983

Selected newspaper articles

Ketcham, Diana. "A Sea Change Where the View Once Ruled." *The New York Times,* May 31, 2001

Richards, Kristen. "Home Swede Home." *archnewsnow.com*

Hopkinson, Natalie, "Making a Debut." *The Washington Post,* September 21, 2001

"A Last Act: Taking Whimsy to School." *The New York Times,* November 26, 1995

"Hail to the Haas." *San Jose Mercury News,* May 7, 1995

"Housing That's Changing the Face of West Berlin." *The New York Times,* April 1988

National AIA Honor Award, 2003: Bo01
"Tango" Housing, Malmö, Sweden

AIA California Council Merit Award,
2003: Bo01 "Tango" Housing, Malmö,
Sweden

Council for New Urbanism Charter
Award, 2002: Tacoma Campus Master
Plan & Phase I, University of Washington

Excellence on the Waterfront Honor
Award, 2002: Bo01 "Tango" Housing,
Malmö, Sweden

La Biennale di Venezia, 2000: Bo01
"Tango" Housing at the Swedish Pavilion
at Mostra Internazionale, Venice, Italy

Årets Stadsbyggnadspris 2001, (The
Year's Building 2001): Bo01 "Tango"
Housing, Malmö, Sweden

American Institute of Architects Honor
Award for Urban Design, 1999: Tacoma
Campus Master Plan & Phase I, Universi-
ty of Washington

American Institute of Architects Honor
Award, 1998: Powell Library, University
of California, Los Angeles

AIA/ALA Library Buildings Award,
1997: Powell Library, University of California, Los Angeles

Los Angeles Business Council Award,
1997: Powell Library, University of California, Los Angeles

Los Angeles Conservancy Award, 1997:
Powell Library, University of California,
Los Angeles

California Governor's Historic Preservation Award, 1996: Powell Library,
University of California, Los Angeles

U.S. Foreign Building Operations,
National Design Competition, First
Prize, 1996: United States Embassy
in Berlin

IIDA Edwin F. Guth Memorial Award of
Excellence for Interior Lighting Design
1996: California Center for the Arts,
Escondido

Lumen West Award for Lighting
Design, 1996: California Center for the
Arts, Escondido

American Concrete Institute, Winner
Architectural Category, 1995: Walter A.
Haas School of Management, Berkeley,
California

United States Institute for Theater
Technology Merit Award, 1995: California Center for the Arts, Escondido

Stucco Manufacturers Association
Bronze Award for Architectural Excel-
lence, 1995: California Center for the
Arts, Escondido

American Institute of Architects
(AIA)/American Association of School
Administrators, Citation, 1994: Walter
A. Haas School of Business Administra-
tion, Berkeley, California

AIA California Council/National Con-
crete Masonry Association Award of
Merit, 1994: Microbiology Research
Facility, University of California, San
Diego

AIA National Interior Architecture
Award of Excellence, 1993: Nativity
Catholic Church

State of Maryland, National Design
Competition, First Prize, 1993: Mary-
land Center for Performing Arts,
University of Maryland

Interiors Magazine 13th Annual Interiors Awards, Best in Institutional
Design, 1992: Nativity Catholic Church

Interfaith Forum on Religion, Art and
Architecture International Architectural Design Honor, 1992: First Church
of Christ, Scientist, Glendale

AIA California Council Urban Design
Award, 1992: Plaza Las Fuentes

AIA California Council Firm of the Year
Award, 1992

AIA Southwestern Oregon Chapter
First Place, Peoples' Choice Awards,
1992: University of Oregon Science
Complex

AIA Southwestern Oregon Chapter
Citation Winner, 1992: University of
Oregon Science Complex

AIA California Council Honor Award,
1992: Yudell/Beebe House

California Institute of Technology, Invited Design Competition, First Place, 1992: Avery House

Arge Karow (Berlin) International Design Competition, First Prize, 1992: Karow-Nord Master Plan

Taiwan National Invited Design Competition, First Prize, 1992: Dong-Hwa University Master Plan

AIA/Sunset Magazine Western Home Awards Award of Merit, 1991-1992: Yudell/Beebe House

American Wood Council National Honor Award, 1991: First Church of Christ, Scientist

AIA San Diego Chapter Honor Award, 1991: Nativity Catholic Church

AIA California Council National Honor Award, 1991: First Church of Christ, Scientist

AIA/American Library Council National Design Award, 1990: Humboldt Library

AIA Los Angeles Honor Award, 1990: Humboldt Library

AIA California Council Merit Award, 1989: House on Point Dume (Anawalt House)

AIA National Honor Award, 1988: Tegel Harbor Housing

AIA California Council Honor Award, 1988: Tegel Harbor Housing

AIA California Council Honor Award, 1988: Carousel Park

City of Santa Monica Mayor's Commendation, October, 1987: Carousel Park

Waterfront Center Excellence on the Waterfront Honor Award, 1987: Carousel Park

State of California Department of Rehabilitation Architectural Design Awards Program, "Building a Better Future Honor Award," 1987: Carousel Park

AIA National Honor Award, 1984: St. Matthew's Church

AIA California Council Merit Award, 1984: St. Matthew's Church

AIA Los Angeles Chapter Merit Award, 1984: St. Matthew's Church

Architectural Record House of the Year, 1981: Rodes House

acknowledgments
photography credits

Acknowledgments

The publication of this book has been no less collaborative than the shaping and crafting of a building. We have enjoyed this as much for its creative process as for the making of an artifact, which we hope can communicate some of the passions, commitments, and hopes we have for architecture.

We feel a special gratitude to the professional colleagues who have helped to contextualize our work. Robert Campbell, distinguished critic and architect has been thoughtful and eloquent in placing our architecture within the context of the contemporary polemic. Jacquelyn Baas, an art historian and Stephen Walrod, a psychotherapist have illuminated aspects of collaboration and habitation that come from the clients' experience. Miller Stevens, an urban planner and colleague has revisited our Karow housing to see, feel, and communicate the current experience of inhabitants. Tina Beebe has been a central creative collaborator in the work. We appreciate not only her exceptional contributions but also her willingness to share insights on her creative process.

Bob Aufuldish of Aufuldish & Warinner has exhibited exceptional care and creativity in the design of this book. He has cared equally about the meaning of the work and the grace of the typography. He has been patient and passionate, constantly refining and renewing the communication of the content. Images Publishing Group, under the direction of Paul Latham and Alessina Brooks, assisted by editor Eliza Hope and graphic designer Rod Gilbert has consistently encouraged our ambition to give *Making Place* a distinct visual quality. Wendy Kohn provided her usual keen critical judgment and editorial assistance on the text. We have been fortunate to have ongoing creative relationships with photographers who communicate the life and spirit of the places we make. Tim Hursley, Werner Huthmacher, and Kim Zwarts have brought vision and understanding to built work. Jim Simmons has helped us visualize places though model photography. Al Forster and Doug Jamieson have brought their talent to the early illustration of work in progress.

Within our office, Janet Sager and Rebecca Bubenas provided thoughtful and attentive guidance from research through coordination of graphic and written material. They exhibited a deep understanding of the values and intentions of the work. Senior Associate James Mary O'Connor contributed his usual enthusiasm and energy in imagining this book as an important representation of the current direction of the firm. Tina Beebe brought her exceptional sense of color and graphics to our in-house work on the book. Ken Kim provided his keen eye and intellect in later stage refinements. Tony Tran continued to be an encyclopedic resource in the collection of photographic images. We appreciate Deenie Yudell for sharing her expertise in both graphics and publication.

Our work develops in a highly inclusive environment and we are greatly appreciative of the personal and professional collaboration of our associates and staff. We often work intensively with associated architectural offices and each experience has enhanced our exploration of architecture and service to our clients. Similarly, our work with numerous consultants has been critical to the success of the work.

We feel exceptionally fortunate to have a diverse range of clients, interested in all scales of architecture. This is a group who has joined us in long-term relationships and friendships, and has been central to the development of a vision for the possibilities of architecture as making place.

These colleagues and collaborators have been abundant and we have endeavored to acknowledge them in our project credits. We thank all of you for your spirit of exploration and collaboration. You've all been partners in understanding, shaping, and inhabiting place.

Photography credits

Morley Baer: 76 (Orinda House), 78

Corbis Images: 169

Dartmouth College: 52 (Dartmouth)

Eames Office: 7 © 2003 Lucia Eames dba Eames Office (www.eamesoffice.com)

Esherick Office: 165

FFNS Architects: 174 (Tango Housing)

Lars Finnström 128-129; 138; 139 (Potatisåkern Housing)

Art Grice: 163

Tim Griffith/Esto: 15

Timothy Hursley: 23; 28-29 (Tacoma); 44 (Yorkin House); 80 (Percival/Westbrook House); 81 (Yudell/Beebe House, Malibu); 146; 148-150; 159 (Baas/Walrod House); 163 (St. Matthew's Church); 167 (Haas School of Business); 186-188; 191-194 (Yudell/Beebe House, The Sea Ranch); 212; 213; 215-221 (Hugh & Hazel Darling Law Library); 241 (Karow)

Werner Huthmacher: 20-21;23-27; 29-31 (Tacoma); 32-35 (Tiergarten); 60-61 (Interdisciplinary Sciences Building); 79 (Tegel Library); 81; 202-205 (Regatta Wharf Housing); 86-89; 93; 95; 96 (Clarice Smith Performing Arts Center); 126; 130-134; 136-138 (Potatisåkern Housing); 170; 172-173; 175-181; 183 (Tango Housing); 202-207 (Regatta Wharf Housing); 228-239 (Manzanita Village Housing); 240-241 (Karow Nord)

Ole Jais: 81; 182; 183 (Tango Housing)

Alan Karchmer: 89-92; 94; 95 (Clarice Smith Performing Arts Center)

John Linden: 218 (Hugh & Hazel Darling Law Library); 222, 224-225 (Horace Mann Elementary School)

LMN Architects: 25; 168 (Tacoma)

Lousiana Museum, Denmark: 83

Machleit + Stepp: 33 (Tiergarten)

Akai Ming-Kae Yang: 168

Jim McHugh: 242-245

Lars Mongs: 135 (Potatisåkern Housing)

Jim Simmons: 108; 110 (United States Courthouse and Federal Building, Fresno); 121 (Beijing Century Center); 125 (United States Air Force Memorial); 142-145 (United States Embassy, Berlin)

Kim Zwarts: 36; 38-43; 45-49 (Yorkin House); 100-107 (Shmuger/Hamagami House); 152-157 (Baas/Walrod House); 184; 190; 195-197 (Yudell/Beebe House, The Sea Ranch)

All other photography courtesy of Moore Ruble Yudell Architects & Planners